M000314472

ELITE

SALES

STRATEGIES

ANTHONY IANNARINO

ELITE

SALES

STRATEGIES

A GUIDE TO

**Being One-Up, Creating Value,
and Becoming Truly Consultative**

WILEY

Published by John Wiley & Sons, Inc., Hoboken, New Jersey.
Published simultaneously in Canada.

For general information on our other products and services or for technical support, please contact our Customer Care Department within the United States at (800) 762-2974, outside the United States at (317) 572-3993 or fax (317) 572-4002.

Wiley also publishes its books in a variety of electronic formats. Some content that appears in print may not be available in electronic formats. For more information about Wiley products, visit our web site at www.wiley.com.

Library of Congress Cataloging-in-Publication Data

Names: Iannarino, Anthony, author.
Title: Elite sales strategies : a guide to being one-up, creating value,
   and becoming truly consultative / Anthony Iannarino.
Description: Hoboken, New Jersey : Wiley, [2022] | Includes index.
Identifiers: LCCN 2021059928 (print) | LCCN 2021059929 (ebook) | ISBN
   9781119858942 (cloth) | ISBN 9781119858966 (adobe pdf) | ISBN
   9781119858959 (epub)
Subjects: LCSH: Sales personnel. | Selling.
Classification: LCC HF5439.5 .I26 2022 (print) | LCC HF5439.5 (ebook) |
   DDC 658.85—dc23/eng/20211228
LC record available at https://lccn.loc.gov/2021059928
LC ebook record available at https://lccn.loc.gov/2021059929

COVER DESIGN: PAUL McCARTHY

SKY10033298_022222

Contents

Foreword

By Charlie Green

MOST BOOKS ON sales follow a predictable pattern—to borrow the philosopher's phrase, they are *teleological.* That is, all writing prior to the author's book boils down to A, B, and C. But now that the truth has been revealed, all roads can be seen as having led to D: *The ___ Sale, ___ Selling, Selling Through ___.* It is a rather egocentric way to present one's thinking, and often doesn't time-travel well (look at the sales bestsellers from 30–40 years ago).

Anthony Iannarino has taken a different approach. He recognizes that there are certain tensions at work in sales, and that these are everlasting and immutable. No methodology or approach is going to transcend them.

Chief among those tensions is the one between the salesperson's desire to *make the sale* and the desire to help the client. How can we be professional and ethical and client focused, all while getting better at bringing money to our own top line? This tension is felt by most salespeople internally, psychologically. It also shows up in approaches and methodologies; for example, *client-focused* easily morphs into the *client focus* of a vulture—focused on the client, all right, but for the sake of the vulture, not the client. Dealing with this tension has actually gotten harder, not easier, by living in a time with instant short-term performance metrics available at every turn, and with countless ways to avoid interpersonal contact.

Another tension is that between ethics and selling, a combination that all too many customers consider an oxymoron. Most salespeople don't like to reflect on this tension, feeling that the addition of ethics to selling will somehow compromise their effectiveness. But the tension is unavoidable; if the salesperson's job is to influence others, and if most salespeople have some reasonable skill at it, then they are in a form of power relationship. Unless you are willing to completely consider clients and customers as mere means to our own ends (and most salespeople actually mean well), then we must consider some aspect of our client relationships and obligations, if only because it's not all about us alone. Most salespeople don't know how to do this (share the pain? bargaining? contracts?), hence it's tempting to ignore.

Anthony doesn't ignore these tensions. In fact, he leads right up front with one of the big ones—power and control—in the form of the concept One-Up. Colloquially, being one up on someone means you have the advantage over them. It's an inherently combative, zero-sum metaphor, that of a winner in a struggle against the putative loser—the customer—who is One-Down.

But One-Up isn't so simple. On the one hand, if you're not One-Up with respect to knowing something of value to the customer that the customer doesn't know, then you're wasting everyone's time. But on the other hand, nobody is *always* One-Up with respect to *every* subject in the world; and if you try to present yourself as being so, you are obviously a bloviating clown whom nobody will believe. Sometimes you're just One-Down. You can try to ignore this, or cover it up with spin, but neither strategy will alter reality; sometimes you're up, and sometimes you're down. Nor should your goal necessarily be simply to be up more often and down less often. It's more about when you should be each, and being conscious and intentional about it. It's a dance, not a winning military campaign.

What Anthony has done in this book is to accept that big tension (and others) as a valid description of reality, and talk about how we as salespeople can navigate the reality-based world of selling for the benefit of all. And "for the benefit of all" is not a throwaway phrase. If all you do is "win" sales "competitions" with your customers, you'll eventually be out of a job. No one likes someone who is solely in it for themselves, and such people get found out pretty quickly. Recognizing this basic truth puts Anthony in a small, rarefied group of sales authors who truly believe that the route to their own success lies in making their customers successful, and in behaving that way consistently and with an eye to the long term, in the face of contrary advice (including from their own sales managers and incentive comp schemes).

So what does it mean to face these tensions head on? Using the big metaphor of One-Up and One-Down, Anthony explores all aspects of sales. While he gives more attention than most to issues of mindset and intent, he also has a foot firmly planted in tactics, implementation, execution, processes, and practical solutions. After all, he has been, and continues to be, very much a practitioner, and the book is chock full not only of solid advice, but also of compelling first- and second-person stories you've never heard before.

This is not primarily a teleological book, but—to borrow the philosophic lexicon once again—a dialectical one. There is yin and yang, always in creative tension, each tension born of prior tensions between older yins and yangs, and each tension resulting in new yins and yangs, which provide an infinitude of more tensions. A great example: The best way to get from One-Down to One-Up on a given issue is to learn from your clients who are One-Up on that issue. The key to getting One-Up is thus to embrace being One-Down and leverage it. As in all cases, it's how we surf the tensions that determines the outcome. To quote that particularly famous philosopher, Spiderman's Uncle Ben (who borrowed it from Voltaire), "with great power comes great responsibility." Getting the sale doesn't take you out of the responsibility game; in fact, playing the larger game is what gets you both power and responsibility.

There is no process, insight, or magic phrase that will truly make you a better salesperson. It's an art, and not a black art but a human one. Navigating the tensions inherent in human relationships is pretty much the same way to navigate the tensions inherent in sales. In fact, they're the same tensions.

Preface

I'VE SPENT MUCH of my career training salespeople to sell better: to understand their clients' needs, to develop insight and business acumen, and most of all, always to trade value for their client's time. Through it all, though, I made myself a promise: I would never provide strategies or tactics that might let one person take advantage of another. I am all too familiar with the high-pressure, hard-sell tactics of the past, and I have seen a number of colleagues train salespeople to do "whatever it takes" to manipulate their prospects.

At a recent conference, for instance, I watched two hustlers maneuver three prospective clients into buying a program that they didn't need by pressuring them in front of a room full of people. I was so upset that I charged out of the room, checked out of my hotel, and caught an early flight home. What I saw was not only unconscionable, but also unnecessary. These men didn't have to rely on dirty tricks. They could have made the sales without forcing their *clients* (read: *victims*) to risk their egos and professional identities simply to decline an offer.

While the idea of being a One-Up salesperson is provocative, at its core it speaks to an ethical obligation to serve others. So, as you read this book, I hope you'll consider both tactics and ethics as you develop your own One-Up position. Use them to serve, to share, and to guide your clients—but most of all, to create value for them because you've been there before. The basic script goes like this: *I know something you don't know. May I share it with you?*

Introduction

People buy from people they trust to make a decision they don't trust themselves to make.

—Chris Beall

Three Miles High and One-Down

I was standing at Basecamp 1 on Mount Everest, where the thinness of the air at 17,000 feet made it hard to breathe. I had no interest in climbing 12,000 more feet to scale the tallest mountain on Earth, but I could not pass up the chance to take some pictures. Unfortunately, I'd suffered from altitude sickness during my entire visit to Tibet: my hands and arms often started tingling, like when your leg falls asleep during a long flight, and more than once I woke up gasping for air. A week's worth of prescription medicine had not done me much good—the tingling was getting worse, and that day it had not stopped for hours. Three miles above sea level, I was becoming concerned.

Soon, even the small hill we were climbing was too much for me to handle. My Sherpa, the guide who arranged and led our

1

trip that day, asked me what was wrong. I breathlessly pushed out the words, "I have altitude sickness. I'm tingling and it's hard to breathe." He replied, "Are you taking altitude medicine?" I pulled the small box of pills out of my pocket and explained that my doctor prescribed them. The Sherpa took one look at the medicine and diagnosed me: "The medicine is what's making you sick. Throw it away, then walk faster so you can get more air into your body." Walk faster? I can barely inch up this hill! But I knew I had to make a choice: Did I trust my guide or my doctor?

Earlier in the day, I had visited my Sherpa's home. On the ground level, donkeys and chickens roamed around on a dirt floor, warmed by a smoke-belching potbelly stove. The outside of the house was covered in yak dung that had been shaped into patties and pressed against the outside walls, each one with an individual handprint of one of the Sherpa's family members. That detail struck me as I pondered my dilemma: I was being advised by a man whose house is covered in yak dung. I was positive that my physician, Dr. Zimmerman, an educated man, used a more, well, conventional insulation to keep his house warm. But I also knew that my doctor had never even been to the Himalayas, let alone Basecamp 1. And while my Sherpa had no formal degrees, he makes a living guiding people up to Everest.

After a long moment, I threw the medicine in a nearby trash can and started walking faster. My lungs burned, but the harder I worked to get up the hill, the better I started to feel. My Sherpa was right: I was getting more air into my lungs. Neither my education nor my doctor's years of medical school could match his knowledge and experience. That expertise put him in the One-Up position, a more valuable resource than a hundred degrees.

What Is the One-Up Position?

The concept of being One-Up, as you might guess, comes from the idea of one-upmanship. The *Oxford English Dictionary* will tell you that one-upmanship is the "technique of gaining a feeling of superiority over another person."[1] But that's not accurate for our purposes. My Sherpa was not advising me because he was trying to show off or feel superior to me. Instead, his knowledge and experience exceeded both mine and my doctor's, so he was confident in both his expertise and how he could help me. A better definition comes from Jay Haley, one of the founders of family therapy at Stanford University's Palo Alto Veteran's Hospital. He also created the strategic approach to psychotherapy. While at Stanford in the early 1950s, Haley was fortunate enough to meet a student (and patient) of psychoanalysis, who had written a book about what he called "the most basic principles of one-upmanship." Haley read the unpublished book, which he recounted in an essay a few years later. In his summary, one-upmanship captures a dynamic present "in any human relationship":

> One person is constantly maneuvering to imply that he is in a "superior position" to the other person in the relationship. This "superior position" does not necessarily mean superior in social status or economic position; many servants are masters at putting their employers one-down. Nor does it imply intellectual superiority as any intellectual knows who has been put "one-down" by a muscular garbage collector in a bout of Indian wrestling. "Superior position" is a relative term which is continually being defined and re-defined by the ongoing relationship.[2]

In this book, we're going to apply the idea of being One-Up to selling more effectively, by using the modern sales approach necessary to help your contacts make effective decisions about how

---

[1] *Oxford English Dictionary* (online), "One-upmanship," 2021.
[2] Jay Haley, quoted in *Jay Haley Revisited*, ed. Madeleine-Richeport Haley and Jon Carlson (New York: Routledge, 2010), p. 6.

they should change to produce better results. At Basecamp 1, my Sherpa was One-Up and I was One-Down—not just because his knowledge and experience far exceeded mine, but because his advice created value for me. If my Sherpa needed help and guidance around a complex sale or sales leadership, I would be in the One-Up position. Generally, the person who needs help and is willing to pay for it is in the One-Down position. You are in the One-Up position when your superior knowledge and experience benefits your clients, which makes your expertise invaluable.

The Ethics of the One-Up Sale

Without a strong ethical underpinning, the powerful strategies and tactics you'll find in this book could easily harm your results. Let's review the interaction I had with my Sherpa. There is no evidence that he thought himself a superior human being, even if his physical abilities and adaptation to the mountain were far greater than mine. He was not competing with me (or with Dr. Zimmerman), nor was he just showing off. Instead, he was offering me help based on his situational knowledge, a type of pattern recognition that only comes from many experiences over time. In this case, he recognized the root of my (unnecessary) suffering: the poor decision I had made to trust my altitude sickness medicine. His One-Up advice forced me to adjust my beliefs and my behaviors, but with the significant benefit of better health outcomes and a far more pleasant visit.

In the world of sales, our prospective clients often struggle to produce results because they made a poor decision, possibly because they didn't fully recognize or understand their circumstances. No part of being One-Up requires you to judge your client for a past mistake or for waiting so long to fix it. Instead, you will use the One-Up approach to help them modify what they are doing and produce the better outcomes they need. The single reason you need to be One-Up is so you can help your contacts be One-Up in their business. This attitude is essential to being a trusted advisor, which as my friend Charlie Green points out, includes being credible, reliable, intimate, and other-oriented. Being One-Up also requires being consultative: providing professional advice that not only helps solve problems but enhances problem-solving in the first place.

In other words, your responsibility to your contacts is to help them be One-Up. Your One-Up advice helps decision-makers and decision-shapers explain their verdict to their teams and build consensus. It allows your contact to be One-Up in internal conversations to make their companies One-Up in their markets, using your recommendations to secure a competitive advantage. You can do all this by helping them make sense of their world, pursue the best decision, and produce the better results they need.

Inventory: Are You One-Down?

While you may need to be temporarily One-Down as your contacts teach you about their company and their industry, staying in that position will harm both you and your clients. To avoid that outcome, you need to be aware of several beliefs and behaviors that would keep you One-Down. Meeting these threats is well worth your time and effort.

- **No Relevant Knowledge.** At the most basic level, you're One-Down when your prospects know more than you do about the decisions they need to make. Knowledge about your own company and its solutions won't dig you out of that hole, since no one hires a guide who knows even less than they do. You don't need to be a know-it-all to correct this imbalance but you do need to be someone who knows "a lot in this area." Eventually, you must become an expert to be One-Up.
- **Not Recognizing the Factors for Decisions.** An inability to recognize the factors that your clients must consider will

make it impossible for you to be One-Up. Decision makers make decisions. You are One-Up when you enable good decisions.

- **No Depth of Understanding.** You might think that the value you create for your clients is found in your solution. You may even pride yourself on your ability to discover a problem. This legacy approach no longer creates a preference to buy from you because it doesn't give your contacts what they really need from you: insight. One of the things that makes you One-Up is your ability to help your client better understand their world and the nature of their problem, so you can create the certainty necessary to move forward in an uncertain world.

- **Not Learning from Your Experiences.** One-Up salespeople recognize that selling is a craft, not just a job. If you're not mindful about your successes and failures, you will have a lot of trouble putting in the effort and care you need. Mastering your craft requires that you learn from your experiences, so you can apply what you have learned in a way that benefits your clients.

- **Outdated Sales Approaches.** Today, how you sell is more important to your success than what you sell. Legacy approaches are too transactional to provide clients the expertise and advice they need, so relying on them puts you One-Down from the start. You are One-Up when your approach creates so much value that your client won't even consider buying from someone else.

- **A Lack of Confidence.** Confidence is necessary to action, both in terms of taking the right actions and of doing anything at all. Without confidence in your own advice and expertise, you can't convince your client that you're the right person to help them improve their results. A client who needs certainty to move forward will avoid buying from a salesperson who creates uncertainty.

- **Desperation for a Deal.** The greater your need to create or win a deal, the easier it is for your client to recognize that you are One-Down. Fearful behavior projects a lack of power and competence, one often stemming from desperation to meet a quota. To be One-Up, your need for a deal cannot exceed your client's need for your consultation. The remedy here is to create so many opportunities that you never need your client's deal more than they need you.
- **Fear of Your Client.** Most salespeople who prospect by email are One-Down, perhaps fearing that making a phone call will somehow harm them. That's an odd fear for a professional salesperson, given that every good thing that ever happens to you in sales is the result of meeting a stranger! You can never be One-Up if you fear your contacts: you will not be able to lead them or provide them with the guidance they need. Instead, you should fear failing them, something that is all but certain if you stay One-Down.
- **Compliance at All Costs.** Fearful salespeople often shrink back from leading their clients. Instead, they will do their very best to be compliant, following the client's lead and taking their orders. Perhaps you started your career as a fast-food cashier, but you don't have to stay there! Being One-Up means leading the client through their decision because you have the better vantage point: you know more than your client about how they should go about pursuing better results.
- **Conflict Aversion.** The customer is not always right: at times, your client will want to do something that will harm their results or prevent them from improving their results. A One-Down salesperson will see the problem but choose to avoid the conflict of pointing it out, passively watching their client make mistakes. But when your client is wrong, they need someone One-Up and unafraid to correct them. Here being One-Up requires that you exercise diplomacy, pointing out the problem without battering your contact's ego.

- **Avoiding Responsibility.** As humans, we're adept at blaming anyone and anything else for our mistakes, including losing a big contract. Avoiding that responsibility is a sure sign of being One-Down: chances are, you lost that deal because you couldn't create the greater value your client needed from you. Being One-Up means accepting the belief that if you are responsible for your wins, you must also be responsible for your losses. Only when you accept both types of responsibility can you look for ways to improve your results.

If these characteristics and practices sound all too familiar, you've got some work to do. That's where the rest of this book comes in: you'll find the strategies, tactics, and some talk tracks that will provide you what you need to be One-Up.

No One Wants a One-Down Partner

Even before you meet, your contacts will measure how valuable you are to them personally and professionally. When they agree to a meeting with you, they're praying that you'll use their time wisely, creating value for them through a helpful conversation. The only way you can make the conversation valuable for you is by making it valuable for your client, starting by avoiding One-Down prospecting.

For example, a salesperson who starts a cold call with "Do you have twenty-seven seconds?" reveals themselves as a joker, not a serious partner. Leading with "Is now a good time?" or "Is now a bad time?" likewise projects that they're One-Down. All of these approaches are fear-based, showing that the salesperson relies on gimmicks or tricks because they can't offer anything more valuable to earn the meeting. How could the tired old agenda of "telling you about our company and the work we are doing with companies just like yours, learn a little bit about you and your company, and discuss how we can help you" be valuable?

The One-Down salesperson is a beggar. They need a meeting more than the client needs their help, and by the widest of margins. After all, the legacy approaches to sales were designed to solve the salesperson's problems. But being One-Up means seeking to solve the client's problems, especially those beyond the scope of your prepackaged solution. The One-Up salesperson believes in their heart that their client is going to benefit from the time they spend with them, a belief that allows them to ask confidently for a meeting and provide a value proposition the client appreciates enough to block off time on their calendar. Here's what that might sound like:

> Good morning! This is Anthony Iannarino with XYZ Widgets. I am calling you today to ask you for a twenty-minute meeting where I can share with you an executive briefing about four trends that will have the most significant impact on manufacturers in the next eighteen to twenty-four months. I'll also provide you with the slide deck and the questions we are asking and answering with our clients, so you can share them with your management team. Even if there is no next step, you'll know what you might start exploring, and you'll know what you might need your team to start putting in place. What do you look like Thursday afternoon?

Why One-Down Salespeople Lose Deals

One of the easiest ways to stay One-Down is refusing the truth that you are the root cause of every one of your problems. If you paid a $35 fee for overdrawing your checking account, it would be ridiculous to claim that the bank made you spend more money than you had. This might sting a little, but you didn't lose that big deal because your prices were too high, your company was too young, or your slide deck didn't have enough fireworks. Your client disengaged with you because you weren't able to stay One-Up by creating value within the confines of the sales conversation. (Oh, and those rambling emails and choked-up voicemails didn't help either.) You can be a wonderful human being, a great parent, an excellent employee, and an incredible karaoke singer without creating enough value to command another meeting.

Like it or not, sales success is individual, not situational. Two salespeople can work at the same company, report to the same manager, sell the exact same product or service to the very same type of customers, and do it all with the exact same pricing, commission, and competitors. But the one who strives to be One-Up will usually find herself at the top of the stacked ranking while her One-Down colleague languishes at the bottom. Perhaps more to the point, she will short-circuit any attempt to avoid responsibility for her losses, instead asking herself what she should have done to win.

One-Up Tactics

I would never leave you with a list of all the ways to be One-Down without providing you a hint of how to become One-Up. The critical outcome of the One-Up approach is that you position yourself as the person best able to help your client make significant decisions around change and improve their results. Chapter 1 explains why the modern sales approach is necessary for being One-Up. In this consultative approach, you don't just ask good questions but also provide professional input and recommendations. To execute this strategy, you must possess greater knowledge and experience than your prospect. In Chapters 2 through 11, I'm going to teach you ten practical tactics to support your One-Up strategy, each in its own chapter.

Chapter 2: The One-Up Sales Conversation: Your Only Vehicle for Value Creation. Of all the strategies you will find here, this may be the most important. The way you create value for your clients and develop a preference to buy from you is exclusively limited to the sales conversation. Your One-Up position makes this possible by helping your clients make better decisions and produce better results through your vantage point, your advice, and your recommendations.

Chapter 3: Insights and Information Disparity. There are some who believe the internet has eliminated the information disparity between the salesperson and their client. This is incorrect, as your clients need more information than ever. However, it's a different kind of information. This strategy will allow you to start teaching your prospects what they need to know to improve their outcomes.

Chapter 4: Supporting Client Discovery. The very nature of discovery has changed. It is less about identifying a need or a problem and more about helping the client discover something about themselves, their business, their decisions, and their results. To be a good guide, you need to be One-Up. But you must also be a good student. There is still much from you to learn from your clients, which is one of the ways you increase your One-Upness.

Chapter 5: Your Role as a Sense Maker. As the world gets increasingly complex, your One-Up position allows you to make sense of it all, by allowing your stakeholders to look through the higher-resolution lens you provide them. Your clients will see something they haven't seen, and something no One-Down salesperson can show them.

Chapter 6: The Advantage of Your Vantage Point. Here you will learn how to guide your clients to better outcomes through your experience helping others on their buyer's journey, preventing them from making mistakes that threaten their future results. Your contacts will find your suggestions far more valuable than anything they have heard from your legacy approach competitors, who still see the decision as a straight line.

Chapter 7: Building Your One-Upness. This chapter offers a road map for identifying and building your insights, as well as an executive briefing that will position you as One-Up from your very first communication—and keep you there all the way to your signing ceremony. Here, you are going to do the work necessary to begin using a modern sales approach.

Chapter 8: One-Up Guide to Offering Advice and Recommendations. As a trusted advisor who is One-Up, you must offer your advice and your recommendations all through the buyer's journey, helping them navigate their actions and decisions. Your advice and your recommendations must be more than "buy my solution from my company." Your counsel will create far greater value.

Chapter 9: The One-Up Obligation to Proactively Compel Change. The antiquated approaches to sales saddle the salesperson with ideas that make them reactive. These ideas prompt practices like discovering problems and qualifying prospects, or the awful tactic of waiting until your client is prepared to buy before you help them. Becoming a trusted advisor means using your "One-Upness" to compel change, preventing your prospective clients from the harm of not changing before they are forced to.

Chapter 10: Triangulation Strategy: Helping Clients Decide While Avoiding Competition. There is a One-Up position that is incredibly powerful and little known, and never taught or trained. This triangulation strategy removes you from the playing field by elevating you to a position above the board, making you no longer just another competitor but the arbiter and ultimate authority. Your contacts will find an advantage in how they understand their decision and their choices.

Chapter 11: Being One-Up Helps Your Clients Change. The ultimate test of your One-Upness is that you cause your client to change. This change is not simply switching partners or solutions; it's a modification of their beliefs, their actions, and their results. The most important changes you need to make occur inside your client's business. When your client makes internal changes, you are One-Up, and your client is all the better for it.

Chapter 12: Advice for Those Who Are Presently One-Down. If you are not presently One-Up, this chapter will speed your development and put you on the path to becoming truly consultative. To achieve One-Upness, you will have to do the work—work worth doing, and work your clients will appreciate.

A Meeting of Equals

In an important sense, you and your client are equals. You are an expert in your field and your client is an expert in theirs. You happen to be in the One-Up position when it comes to helping your contacts improve their results. Your client is an expert in their industry and their business, making them One-Up in these areas. This combination of One-Upness and One-Downness allows you to work together to produce the best results, solve problems, address challenges, and take advantage of opportunities.

Being One-Up isn't about conflict, trickery, or dominance. On the contrary, it's about creating an obligation to serve your clients by becoming the kind of salesperson they need—one with the expertise and experience to provide them with good counsel, advice, and recommendations. Like teachers, doctors, and even Sherpas, One-Up salespeople enable their clients to make better decisions and reach better outcomes. It's not something you can fake, as your client will know within minutes whether you can back up your claims. You are much better off doing the work of becoming One-Up: recognizing where you are One-Down, then learning from others' guidance and expertise to help you level up.

1

The Modern Sales Approach

The illiterate of the 21st century will not be those who cannot read and write, but those who cannot learn, unlearn, and relearn.

—Alvin Toffler

PROFESSIONAL SELLING HAS evolved over the past 75 years or so and using the modern sales approach is the best way to show that you're One-Up. Despite this, two older approaches, legacy laggard and legacy solutions, are still practiced. One reason you may be One-Down is because you are using a legacy approach to selling, one that is ill-equipped to create better outcomes for your clients. Here, we'll look at why the legacy approaches can hold you back, and how the modern approach can help you become One-Up.

The Legacy Laggard

Even the most recent strategies and tactics you find in the legacy laggard approach are now more than fifty years old, with some elements dating all the way back to the 1920s. They're built on the concept of information disparity, the idea that because your client was lacking information about your company's products or services, they needed to meet with a salesperson to learn what is available. As you will learn in Chapter 3, this disparity allowed salespeople to take advantage of the customers.

The fact that the prospect needed to buy something the buyer was selling made the interaction transactional, like many business-to-consumer purchases, but transactional models don't create the right level of value for B2B sales. Legacy laggard salespeople are trained to find "the decision-maker," the single person with the authority to decide to sign a contract and ensure payment, overcome their objections, and make the sale. That process started by answering "why us," with the salesperson attempting to prove credibility by talking about their company's strengths and history to persuade the prospective client to buy from them.

Because prospects in the 1950s and 1960s couldn't simply browse the company website, the salesperson also provided them with particulars of their company's products and services. The value of the conversation was limited to the products and services the sales organization provided, as they were central to making a sale. In fact, if you still start your sales conversation by talking about your company and your products, that strategy is pure legacy laggard. One of the main tenets of the legacy approach was to refuse to provide "free consulting," an idea that not only reduces your value but prevents you from being One-Up.

Legacy Solutions

As the environment changed and companies demanded more from their *suppliers* or *partners*, labels that suggested a greater obligation than one might reasonably expect from a *vendor*, the new legacy solutions approach provided greater value to both the customer and the sales organization. The major shift in this period is best illustrated by the idea of discovery. Instead of the salesperson just sharing information about products and services, the first conversation morphed into a series of questions designed to find the prospect's *dissatisfaction*, their *pain point*, or their *hot button*. These conversations were—and are— still more valuable than the legacy laggard approaches. If your sales conversations focus on finding a problem that fits your company's solution, you're still using a legacy solution approach.

Salespeople who used a legacy solution approach still tried to answer "why us," but they added "why our solution" to the mix. As solutions grew more complex and became more critical to a company's business results, the decision-maker gave way to the buying committee or task force, the group of people charged with deciding what to buy and from whom. Not only would the salesperson have to overcome objections, but they'd also be required to provide proof that the solution would work for this particular client.

In a legacy solution approach, the solution is the value, and the salesperson provides value by solving the client's problem, getting us about halfway to an approach that is consultative.

Before we go any further, please don't worry if your approach is cobbled together from both legacy approaches. I used both models myself early in my career, and they were genuinely useful before rapid market changes caused me to adapt a more modern approach, focusing on creating enough value to win deals.

The Modern Approach

The modern approach is consultative, requiring much more of the salesperson. Modern contacts, stakeholders, decision-makers, and decision-shapers need salespeople to create greater value (read: more help). No client finds value in a conversation that doesn't help them improve their decisions and their results.

The focus of the sales conversation is no longer "why us" or "why our solution." Instead, it's now about "why change" and "why now." Instead of relying on your company and your solutions for your credibility, trusting you can create value in the sales conversation, the modern approach requires arming yourself with insights and a certain perspective on what your client needs to do to improve their outcomes.

Because you already know what problems the companies you call on are experiencing, instead of helping the client to identify a need or a problem that needs solving, the modern approach starts by helping your contacts understand their world—one often marked by dissonance stemming from the constant, accelerating, disruptive change in their environment. By explaining the nature of their contacts' challenges, the One-Up salesperson helps them recognize the need to do something different and provides them with the ability to improve their results. It's important to note that none of these outcomes require you to mention your company, your products, your services, or your "solutions."

When your clients need significant change, that decision isn't going to come from a traditional decision-maker or a buying committee. The larger and more strategic the initiative, the more you are going to need something closer to organizational consensus. Instead of objections, you find your contacts with real concerns that speak to their uncertainty, which often paralyzes them and prevents them from moving forward. Being One-Up is required to resolve those concerns and create certainty around doing what is necessary to improve your client's position.

As the (One-Up) person best positioned to guide the (One-Down) client to the better results they need, you must lead them. We'll cover some leadership tactics later, but for now, know that your insights include which conversations your stakeholders need to have to make the best decision for their company. You can think of this as an *agile, facilitated, needs-based buyer's journey*. While the legacy approaches treated the sales conversation as linear, a straight line from Target to Closed/Won, the modern approach accepts that both sales conversations and decision-making are now nonlinear, requiring the agility enabled by being One-Up.

True Confessions of a Legacy Salesperson

I started making cold calls for a nonprofit when I was fifteen years old. After two weeks, I found a much better job at a skating rink, so I quit. During that two-week period, I had scheduled two events—two more than all of my coworkers combined. There is no way that I was especially good at the work; my success was due to my work ethic and my ability to suffer without complaint.

Not too many years later, when I was forced into an outside sales role, I was taught and trained to present my company by walking the client through a huge binder that was designed to answer both classic legacy questions: "why us" and "why our solution." I literally read the binder to the poor, suffering souls who were too polite to throw me out of their office. One prospect was basically catatonic when I left her office. I really hope she had a good health plan.

When the $4 billion company I worked for decided to train me, they taught me to ask my prospective clients for a single order, the old "get the camel's nose under the tent" strategy. (It's cold in the desert at night, and when you allow a camel to put his nose under the tent, you end up with a not-so-cuddly animal sleeping next to you.) In a role play, however, I tried to convince the regional vice president to give me all of her orders. After the exercise, I was taken into another room and told that I would no longer be allowed to participate in the training. The regional vice president was concerned that I was "scaring the salespeople who were afraid to ask for an order." My manager laughed at the situation, as we had fun taking over entire accounts, preferring to acquire clients instead of orders. It would take me nine full years of sales before I was able to help my clients adjust more than the name of their supplier. Eventually, though, I found my way to One-Up, and I haven't looked back.

Being One-Up is vital simply because there is no reason for a client to ever take advice from someone in the One-Down position, especially when it comes to making important decisions and pursuing better results. What value is a salesperson who knows less than the client they are trying to help? In Nancy Duarte's excellent book *Resonate*, she suggests that your client is Luke Skywalker while you are Yoda. Your client is the hero, albeit one who is rather clueless, presently inadequate for their mission, and a bit of a fixer upper. You, however, have greater experience and the ability to provide the help your clients need.

Personally, I prefer Obi-Wan Kenobi to Yoda; maybe it's the white beard. In either case, you have to provide insights that allow your client to succeed in their mission. The starting point for making a One-Up sale is demonstrating your expertise in the sales conversation with your prospective client, leading with the insights your contacts need. You need not worry about sharing your insights or providing risky "free consulting," as it's far riskier to pursue a legacy approach. Besides, you are going to teach your client everything they know, but not everything you know.

How Your Client Knows You Are One-Down

There are a number of obstacles to becoming One-Up. The first obstacle is an unawareness of the plan necessary to execute the strategies and tactics that make up this approach. Without a complete approach to the One-Up strategy, it is more difficult to execute. Your client will recognize your One-Downness by your approach. When you open a conversation by sharing information about your company, for example, you have already demonstrated that you have nothing more valuable to share. When what you share creates no value for your client's future results, you are One-Down.

The desperate attempt to build rapport at the beginning of a conversation with your prospective client also broadcasts your One-Down desperation. The new rapport in sales is a business conversation. The more you need a deal, the more you present yourself as One-Down. If you are really desperate, you might be Two-Down, knowing even less than those who are One-Down. The nature of your conversations and your questions also provides evidence of your One-Downness. When you ask your client questions about the problems they are having, you prove you are an amateur. How could you not already know what kind of problems and challenges your client might be experiencing? And even beyond that, not starting with a theory about why, what, and how your prospect should change means you are One-Down.

Here is a simple test to determine if you are One-Down: Does the client benefit from the conversation more than you do?

There are other tells that prove you are in the One-Down position when compared to your contacts. The more you comply with a process that is being driven by your contacts or their company, the more certain it is that you are One-Down. When your prospective client sends you an RFP and you respond, you have shown that you are subservient, servile, compliant, and worst of all, One-Down.

By the way, the One-Up approach to an RFP would start with a call to the person who sent it so you can explain that there is no way you can answer their questions and still show them how companies like yours help clients with better results. Then, to ensure they understand they are One-Down, you ask them a question they can't answer: "Is there a reason you are trying to do this the way we stopped doing it four years ago?" Before they can answer, add, "How do you want us to document our approach?" Congratulations, you are now One-Up. Your contact is now concerned about what they don't know, and they now know someone who understands what they are missing. Worst-case scenario, you get invited to present.

Mistakes to Avoid

There are a few common mistakes when flexing your One-Upness, and we might as well get the biggest one out of the way before we move forward. The worst possible thing you can do when using the One-Up strategy is to come off as arrogant. You want to avoid being a know-it-all and instead be seen as someone who knows a lot in this specific area. You don't want your client to think that you believe you are somehow superior to them as a human being. The human beings you call on don't ever need to feel as if they are One-Down outside of the decision you are helping them make. If you are an Alpha, any hint of arrogance is going to be treated as a challenge by another Alpha. It is also going to be recognized by non-Alphas as desperation to be important. The best way to execute this strategy is to recognize that you are One-Up in the areas where you have more knowledge and experience than your client, while they are One-Up in a dozen or more areas where you are One-Down. It's humbling, I know.

Treat everyone as if they are smart but lacking some information that you can offer them to improve their decision-making and better future outcomes. One of the ways to soften your approach is to ask for permission to share ideas with your clients, ensuring that you don't poke the ego of someone who is used to being in a dominant position. You might also ask your contact to share their perspective with you, something that acknowledges their authority. Remember, you are equals.

The greatest risk to your success with this approach is to believe that you can learn nothing from your client to understand how best to serve them—and your future clients. A large factor that makes you One-Up is how much you have learned from your clients. Those who wish to teach should start by committing to learn. You must recognize when you need to be One-Up, as well as when you are—and need to be—One-Down. You better occupy the space of One-Up by descending to the One-Down position when someone else is One-Up and can help you see something that was unavailable to you. You are going to need to become an expert to maintain the One-Up position where you know more than your clients. Your client is in the One-Up position when they are sharing with you how things work in their company. In this case, your One-Down position allows you to take in new information that will be critically important to you later, when you find yourself One-Up again.

The Virtuous Circle of Increasing One-Upness

You are an expert in what you sell, and if you are not, I hope you are on your way to becoming one; it will change your results and your life. Your client is an expert in their industry and their role, meaning they are One-Up in those areas. By providing your client with the insights and information they are lacking as it pertains to the better results they need, you help them become One-Up—not over you, but over others who know less. The same is true for you. When your client helps you understand their business, their industry, their overall strategy, and a dozen other topics that close the gaps in your knowledge and experience, you are less One-Down and more One-Up, even if you lack the expertise of someone who spent their life in their industry. You know more than you did, and it's likely you know more than someone who isn't trying not to be perpetually One-Down.

There is no reason that you should worry about teaching your client what they need to know to be One-Up. They are not likely to surpass your One-Upness because they will not be able to acquire your experience selling what you sell. Your experience is deeper and wider than your clients who make a given buying decision once every few years at most. You help clients and prospects make those decisions every day. If you sell in different verticals, you know things that other people don't because you spend time learning from your contacts, but you recognize that you lack the expertise of your clients in their industry.

How Being One-Down Makes You One-Up

One of the ways you improve your ability to be One-Up is by being One-Down when you need to be. In one of my first jobs as a field salesperson, I called on large distribution centers in my territory of Columbus, Ohio. It was a target-rich environment, and I had homed in on a number of very large prospects, each one spending millions of dollars with companies in my industry. Having won one of the largest retail distribution centers in the city, I was learning how best to take care of their needs. My main client was a seasoned veteran of the business, and he invited me to sit in on his planning meeting, an indication that he favored me over my competitors.

The conversation I was listening to was in a language I didn't speak. First, the managers and leaders used a lot of acronyms that made no sense to my ears. Second, they used lot of jargon. While I didn't yet have the concept of being One-Down, I felt it. I was lost. When I left the meeting, I asked my main contact to help me make sense of what I heard, especially the term *throughput*. It's not difficult to guess the meaning of the word, but for this group, it was a math equation. He patiently explained to me that the throughput was a calculation based on how much product they shipped divided by the cost of their labor. They had goals around throughput. He showed me how they kept score on a spreadsheet. A few weeks later, I walked into a different prospective client's distribution center and asked my main contact what their throughput numbers were like during their peak season. He was stunned by the question, as no one else in my role would have known to ask. There is no way I was One-Up when it came to running a distribution center, but I was One-Up on any and all of my competitors. Without knowing that I was being taught to be One-Up, I was gaining a competitive advantage by asking my client to educate me about their business, correcting my One-Downness.

Learning From Your One-Up Client

There are many things you need to know to successfully help your client change and produce the outcomes they need to be successful. But at least in these three areas, you need your client to help you understand what you need to know and how to use that knowledge to help them succeed.

Their Industry   Unless you have worked in your prospective client's industry, your client is certain to know more about their industry than you. What you want to be is an expert on the line where your industry and your client's industry come together. You are already an expert in your industry, and you understand what's on your side of that line. Because your client is an expert in their industry, they have the knowledge and experience to be able to help you understand their side. Every interaction with a stakeholder provides you with an opportunity to be tutored by experts in a specific industry. When your contacts tell you how their business works, how challenges show up in their world, and what the optimal change might look like for them, you have gained information that allows you to be better prepared for future conversations with other clients or prospects. In a conversation with a new prospect, you are starting out less One-Down than you might have been had you not learned from your previous clients.

What's even better is discovering that some companies have beliefs and ideas that conflict with other companies in the same industry. When you are aware that some approach works in some scenarios and fails under different circumstances, you have situational knowledge to understand what works, when it works, and what conditions need to be present for something to be true. Every industry has a number of things that differentiate it from other industries. Your client can teach you how they think about their business and their industry, providing you with the context needed to understand why they do certain things in a certain way. Industries also tend to have a set of concepts and a vocabulary that is all their own. You want your client to teach you how to think about their business and how to speak their language. You want to sound and feel like an insider, someone who is "one of us." Every interaction with a contact inside your prospective client's account is an opportunity to learn something that will benefit you now and in the future.

What Your Contacts Believe Your contacts are operating based on certain assumptions, some of which are false. Those false assumptions may not have started out incorrect, but they have outlived their value as the world changed. It's much easier to help people adjust their no-longer-accurate assumptions when you understand what assumptions they have now. We are laying down two sets of tracks here: the beliefs that prevent your client from producing the results they need, as well as the things they believe that are true. Both tracks are valuable to you in helping them improve their results.

The reason stakeholders don't love your slide deck presentation when you propose an initiative or project is that they prefer to grill you with not-so-hypothetical hypotheticals to ensure what you propose will work for them. In previous conversations, you might not have captured all of these questions and the responses to the questions you ask to gain greater clarity—organizing your knowledge, increasing your knowledge and experience, moving ever closer to being an expert. Now you know better.

Navigating Their Company   There is one area where you are no match for your contact when it comes to being One-Up: how things work in their company. Unless your contact is new to their company or their role, they know how things get done inside their world. There is a lot of tribal knowledge inside any group of people that spend most of their waking hours together. Your contacts are going to know where all the landmines are buried. Your lack of knowledge about how to traverse this ground makes you One-Down and open to the types of mistakes that can cause you problems as you help your client pursue the results they need. You don't know that any criticism about Jimmy's sacred cow is going to lose his support. Unless you are able to pick it up in meetings, you have no idea that Jenny has had all she can take from Jimmy being so averse to the change she believes is necessary. The people who have a map to this terrain are your contacts, many of whom lack formal authority but have tremendous insight about their peers and how best to pursue change inside their company. Later, your map is going to be helpful to you and your contacts, putting you in the One-Up position because you will know more than your client.

One way to remain forever in the One-Down position is to ignore all of the things you see and hear when you are meeting with your clients. You can work toward being One-Up by learning from your clients. I promise you that by the end of this book, you will be One-Up, and you will value every client conversation in a new way.

2

The One-Up Sales Conversation: Your Only Vehicle for Value Creation

A single conversation across the table with a wise man is better than 10 years' mere study of books.
—Henry Wadsworth Longfellow

BEING ONE-UP MEANS embracing a new sales conversation, one very different from those you've had with past contacts. The new conversation requires more of you. You are responsible for providing what your clients need from the conversation, not just for paving the way to your own success. You cannot occupy the One-Up position using tired, outmoded, and antiquated approaches to sales. Nor can you help your clients move from One-Down to One-Up if you cannot transfer your insights to the decision-makers and decision-shapers you serve.

You've probably gone through entire sales meetings where nothing you shared seemed to register with your prospective client. The reason you didn't command your contact's attention, let alone compel them to move forward, is because the information you provided wasn't what your contact needed. Your approach to professional selling must evolve, as you work to help your clients improve their results. When your approach doesn't provide value, your clients will look elsewhere for help.

This focus on value is a response to our increasingly complex economic and cultural environment, one that brings constant, accelerating, disruptive changes. What made "the good old days" so good was their greater stability. The future didn't look too different from the past. But the complexity your contacts experience causes a sense of dislocation and greater uncertainty, requiring a sales conversation that helps them make sense of their world and move forward with confidence and certainty. Rather than parroting a commoditized script, especially during discovery, being One-Up means leading a different conversation, one that speaks to needs that One-Down salespeople rarely even recognize.

The Commoditization of the Sales Call

The discovery call has been fully and completely commoditized. We are using the word "commodity" as economists define it. A commodity is fungible (meaning interchangeable) and the market has no concern about who produced it. One is as good as the next. That is the bad news. The good news is that anytime something is commoditized, it's easy to create the meaningful differentiation that would transform it into something people care about because it is more valuable.

Let's look at a typical sales call. The salesperson walks into the client's office and starts with a little small talk, hoping to create the rapport that would make them more comfortable. They offer the client an agenda that starts by sharing information about their company, after which they suggest that they'll ask some questions to "learn a little about" the client and their company. With that agenda firmly established, the salesperson predictably brags about their company and the clients they serve, hoping to prove that they are credible before launching into questions designed to identify the client's pain point. Following this training is the key to their ultimate goal: proposing their solution.

Imagine how familiar this script must be to your prospective clients, most of whom have experienced the traditional sales call dozens or hundreds of times. Each salesperson who steps into their office or conference room treats them to effectively the same conversation. A client once shared with me that every salesperson he met with could easily sell their competitor's product or service by swapping out the company name and logo on their slide deck. The salespeople themselves differed only by height and hair color. It's no wonder your contacts are short on patience!

When there is no difference between one meeting and the next, that conversation is a commodity. Producing yet another carbon copy of your competitor's commoditized conversation makes you One-Down in the worst way possible.

The Single Vehicle for Value Creation Is the Sales Conversation

The new sales conversation has no room for anything that doesn't improve your client's ability to decide for their company and their future results.

In *Eat Their Lunch: Winning Customers Away from Your Competition*, I point out that you, the salesperson, are the value proposition: not your company, not your solution, and not anything external. You walk into a prospect's office alone, and you are solely responsible for what you do with the gift of their time. You have to create enough value for your client that they agree to move forward with you. Salespeople who are One-Down believe value is something their company and their solution delivers after the sale, not something they deliver during the sales conversation. No matter how good your solution is, its benefits are strictly theoretical during the sales conversation. Thus, your clients must use their sales conversation experience with you—including the One-Up insights and advice you offer—to determine whether to buy from you.

The One-Up strategy and its ten supporting tactics all exist inside the single vehicle available to you to win deals. That vehicle is the sales conversation, and it is where you establish your One-Upness by creating massive value for your prospective clients, removing them from the One-Down position in which you find them. To make this critical One-Up strategy practical, tactical, and actionable, we will use a thought experiment to distinguish between One-Up and One-Down sales conversations.

Here's the scenario: You have been granted a meeting with your dream client, one who spends an enormous amount of money in your category. They're perfect for you, and you're excited by the opportunity to meet with them. However, before you may enter the room where your contact is waiting, you must agree to these rules:

1. You may not mention your company's name. Any mention of who you work for or what your company does will cause

you to be immediately escorted out of the meeting, with no appeal. There are no exceptions or second chances.

2. You must not mention any of your clients, including any testimonials or any results you have generated for and with companies you serve. A single mention of a client's name or a hint at the results you created will cause two large bodyguards to pick you up by your arms, escort you off the premises, and stuff you in your car.

3. You are prohibited from mentioning your product, your service, or your solution. Any mention of what you sell will be considered a breach of your agreement with your dream client, resulting in the termination of the meeting. Your contact is not interested in hearing about what you sell.

4. Any attempt to develop rapport with your contact is a violation that will end your meeting and will bar you from ever speaking to the contact again. Your contact values their time and only gives it to people who use it wisely, not strangers who try to make the conversation personal.

5. You may ask no questions that elicit your client's "dissatisfaction," their "pain points," or their "hot button." A single question about "what's keeping them up at night" will end the meeting, the trap door underneath your chair will open, and you will find yourself in the underground parking garage.

6. You have 25 minutes to meet with your contact. If you succeed in using the time wisely, your contact will schedule an hour-long meeting with you to explore change.

This thought experiment provides several challenges, each of which is easily solved by being One-Up. These same challenges will eliminate the One-Down salesperson within minutes, because it removes all the legacy tricks and talking points they have been provided.

The first challenge you face is how best to open a sales call without mentioning your company's name. The One-Down salesperson relies heavily on their company to create credibility. The need to rattle off facts about your company in early conversations is proof positive you are One-Down. The need to share the names and results you have created for your existing clients points to an attempt to establish credibility, more evidence you are One-Down. Since any attempt at personal rapport finds you in breach of your agreement, that strategy is off the table too. Pointing at things external to the conversation to bolster your credibility projects your One-Downness. Instead, you have to establish your credibility through the sales conversation, by demonstrating your relevance and your ability to make sense of the client's world.

Once you figure out how to open the sales call, you have to fill twenty-five minutes with content your client finds valuable. The rules prevent you from sharing any information about your product or your services, removing those topics from consideration. The approach that most legacy salespeople use is to ask questions designed to elicit their client's "pain," this being the key to shoving their quick-fix solution in front of their client. Being One-Up means leading a different conversation, one designed to create greater value for your client in areas where they need greater help. There is a time and place for the traditional conversations, like "why us," but those discussions occur much later, and only when they're valuable to an outcome you need to create for your client.

How to Command Your Contact's Attention

In a meeting with a large prospect, I was ushered into a room with four people from his team. When the decision-maker walked into the room a couple of minutes later, he sat down and said, "Anthony, tell me about your company and what you guys do." Recognizing that he already knew what we did, I responded, "I am afraid that would be a terrible waste of your time."

He said, "No, I'd really like to learn about you guys." Saying no to simple, early client requests can give them an unpleasant impression of what it's like to work with you. So, instead of resisting his request, I pivoted and said, "The best way to describe who we are and what we do is to share the things we care about." At that point I started providing insights about complex developments I knew were causing his company to experience poor results. Armed only with a legal pad and zero PowerPoint slides, I explained the forces and trends causing his problems, something I knew he was struggling with without having to ask.

One hour and seven minutes into the meeting, the decision-maker excused himself from the table, leaving me with his four employees. The employee sitting across from me asked me, "How'd you do that?" I must have looked confused, because she clarified: "How did you keep him in this room for over an hour? He has never spent over five minutes with a salesperson." I answered, "I think he was enjoying the conversation." The truth is that he stayed because the conversation was valuable to him. If he found the content of our conversation a waste of his time, he would have left much earlier, apparently something that a lot of One-Down salespeople got to experience. Busy professionals actively avoid One-Down conversations, the kind that do nothing to help them make better decisions and reach better outcomes.

How a One-Up Salesperson Creates Value

To craft a One-Up conversation that creates value for your clients and prospects, you first have to recognize what might help them move from their One-Down position to a One-Up position.

In any organization, leaders make decisions. For important decisions that can create a better future state for the company, they look for help from people who are One-Up as it pertains to the results they need. Remember, people buy from people whom they trust to decide more than they trust themselves. They won't look for mission-critical advice and recommendations from a person who is One-Down, one who knows even less than they do. When you recognize that your recommendations actually make you the decision-maker, you'll understand why they buy from one person and not another.

Spending time talking about your company, your solutions, the results you have produced for others, or even the recent heroics of the local sports team—especially early in the conversation—identifies you as a time waster instead of a value creator. The rapport-building that was once found at the beginning of the conversation now occurs at the end. The new rapport is a business conversation, one enabling effective decision-making and better future results. Here are two specific ways you can create value for your contacts and clients in that process.

Understanding Their World in the Context of a Decision

As a professional salesperson, you spend all of your time helping your clients improve their results, while your clients only occasionally make a decision that you help others make every day. When you open a sales call with an executive briefing, you immediately present yourself as One-Up. There are several categories of insights you might use to help improve your client's position, but in this early conversation focus on the forces, trends, and factors that contextualize and ultimately enable good decisions. Not only does this help your client understand what's going on in their world and why they should care, but it also helps compel them to change in response.

Based on my conversations with salespeople, there are two common concerns about beginning your sales conversation with a briefing. First, you might worry that your client already fully knows the trends and factors you might share with them. Even if you do find a contact who already understands the forces that should inform their decisions, remember: You are providing this briefing to establish that you are an expert and that you are paying attention to what's important on behalf of your clients. Your provocative perspective is helpful. The second concern is that your client knows more than you. This is also rare, but again, you still score points for being aware of the forces and trends that matter to them. You sound more like a peer than a salesperson. Most leaders have an intellectual humility, surrounding themselves with people who can help improve their view and enable good decisions.

A different problem arises, however, when you open a conversation with a client who believes that they are already One-Up on this topic. There, you need language that prevents their ego from hindering their learning. Here, you can simply open the conversation by saying, "Would it be okay if I shared this briefing with you? I am certain you are tracking these same trends, and it would help me to get your perspective on how much these things are showing up in your world." There is no benefit to making this client feel One-Down, especially when doing so would engage their ego-defense mechanisms. Instead, you want to provide a conversation that diplomatically starts them on the path to being One-Up.

Recognizing Forces and Their Impact on Results

The legacy approaches to sales would have you spend a good bit of time identifying your client's pain points. This is a One-Down approach to sales, as it indicates that despite (allegedly) helping your clients produce better results every day, you are clueless as to what challenges your prospective client will likely experience. Why on earth would you call another human and ask them for a meeting about change if you didn't already have a strong theory as to their challenges and the better results they need? Starting with this theory lets you both teach your client and learn from them simultaneously.

Exploring change with your stakeholders means helping them understand the implications of certain factors critical to their decision-making and their future results. Specifically, your opening should position you as an expert with the ability to compel change and a preference to buy from you. How are you opening a sales call now, and how does it create value for your clients? Likewise, a One-Up salesperson can control the process, leading the client and gaining commitments to all the conversations necessary to produce better results. How much control do you have over the process now and what competencies do you have in place to prevent deals from stalling? Answering these questions honestly and thoroughly will help you identify gaps in your performance, the first step to being more One-Up in your approach.

Things to Stop Doing

- **Starting with "Why Us."** This One-Down approach is out of sync with your contact's needs. They don't need an answer to this question early on and it feels as if you are pitching the client (mostly because you are). This approach makes you a bad first date, spending your time talking about your company when your client hopes you are there to help them improve their outcomes.
- **Personal Rapport-Building.** You are One-Down when you try to create rapport in hopes of being liked. We have to carefully thread the needle here. In general, the new rapport-building is a business conversation in B2B sales. After the meeting, if your client wants to have a personal conversation, there is no reason not to work on a personal relationship to accompany your commercial relationship. However, different locations may mean different customs. If your territory is one where your clients expect a personal conversation before the business conversation, don't ignore the cultural norms.

- **Commoditized Discovery.** As I noted earlier, the discovery call has been commoditized. The One-Down goal of discovery is to identify a "gap," a "pain point," or a "source of dissatisfaction." If that's all you're doing, you are repeating the same conversation your client has had dozens or hundreds of times. It's not that these things are not important, but that you need to create more value before you get there.
- **Differentiating Your Company and Your Solution.** When every salesperson begins a conversation by sharing information about their company or their solution, doing the same thing won't differentiate you. Approaching the sales call this way means starting from a One-Down position with a person who needs you to be One-Up. Your conversation is the only way to provide real differentiation.
- **Following the Client's Lead.** There is a certain variety of faux sales experts who suggest that you should allow your client to tell you what comes next. These poseurs would have you occupy the position of One-Down, never leading and never taking charge. But allowing someone who rarely travels the path they are on to lead the journey is negligence at best, and a dereliction of duty at worst.

Things to Start Doing

- **Establish Yourself as a Potential Strategic Partner.** The more you present as a One-Up expert who can cover the gaps in your client's knowledge and experience, the more you look like a strategic partner. The more you brief clients and keep them up to date on what's important, the more they'll come to rely on you to take care of that part of their success.
- **Compel Change and Provide Context.** There is a subtle but critical difference between the One-Down elicitation of a client's pain points and the One-Up approach of teaching them why they have those pain points. In the first case, you

are trying to force your solution into the conversation, and in the second you are helping your client recognize the reason they're struggling. In the first you are asking for information; in the second, you are providing information and insights that provide you and your client even more information. Decision-makers and leaders already want better results; they just struggle to find people who can help.

- **Differentiate in the Sales Conversation.** The only effective way you create differentiation is through the sales conversation. The differentiation you need to provide comes from your insights and your ability to make sense of your client's world, providing them with a higher-resolution lens through which to view their decisions and their future results.
- **Facilitate a Needs-Based Buyer's Journey.** Much of the new sales conversation is about the One-Up approach of filling the gaps in your prospective client's knowledge and experience. By recognizing what your client needs, you can better provide them with information, insight, and recommendations to ensure they succeed. Remember: there is no buyer's journey; there are only buyers' journeys. You need to lead.

Starting the New Sales Conversation

Let's return to our thought experiment with the rather stringent conversational contract. Here, I will demonstrate the One-Up approach to starting the new conversation, pretending you are the prospect who's gifted me with 25 minutes of your time.

Thank you for your time. Unless you have any objection, I'd like to start by sharing with you the current state of sales today and some factors that prevent sales organizations and salespeople from producing the results they are capable of.

- According to HubSpot's 2020 "Not Another State of Marketing Report," only 29 percent of buyers want to learn more about products by talking to salespeople.[1]
- Forrester reports that 68 percent of B2B buyers prefer to do their own online research rather than interacting with sales reps. This is because sales reps provide mostly useless material (cited by 57 percent of buyers) that is "focused more on style than substance" (cited by 58 percent).[2]

One thing that we have noticed is that it is more difficult to obtain meetings when the salesperson doesn't promise to provide the client with something of value. We also see an uptick in meetings when the salesperson promises to provide value even if the client doesn't buy anything, a sort of risk reversal that makes it easier for their contact to agree to a meeting. This is strong evidence that decision-makers are looking for a different conversation.

- Gartner's research shows that decisions are also made before contacting salespeople. Their research has shown that 57 percent of clients' decisions are made before they speak to a salesperson.[3]

The implication for salespeople is that it is increasingly important to meet with prospective clients early, an approach we call Year Zero. Because buyers are doing work on their own, qualifying the way you might have in the past means missing opportunities.

---

[1] HubSpot, "Not Another State of Marketing Report," 2020.
[2] Forrester, "Beyond The Lead: How Content Marketing Builds Lasting Relationships" webinar, 2018.
[3] Gartner, "The Power of the Challenger Sales Model," August 17, 2019.

- Buying cycles are growing longer. There is evidence that 75 percent of deals take four months,[4] with nearly half taking more than seven months.[5]
- Between 2009 and 2014, sales cycles increased by 22 percent, and that trend has continued. According to CSO Insights, the percentage of sales cycles taking more than one year increased from 10 percent to 18 percent between 2013 and 2019.[6]

One factor that seems to cause longer cycles times is the buyers' need to acquire consensus inside their own company. Even though we have recognized this trend, most sales organizations haven't developed the methodologies to provide their clients the help they need.

- The B2B sales cycle has become so complex that about 46 percent of sales representatives expect to miss their sales quota; the win rate is about 47%.[7]
- According to a study by ValueSelling Associates, Inc., and Selling Power, which asked over 300 B2B salespeople about their quotas, 69 percent of the B2B salespeople say they won't reach their quota due to the lack of enough leads in their pipeline.[8]

---

[4] CSO Insights, "Selling in the Age of Ceaseless Change: 2018–2019 Sales Performance Study," 2018.
[5] Sheryll Poe, "Your Guide to B2B Sales: Steps and Tips for Successful Sales," The Blueprint, a Motley Fool Service, December 8, 2020.
[6] CSO Insights, "2019 Sales Performance Report," 2019, 16.
[7] Ibid.
[8] ValueSelling Associates, "The Three Keys to Sales Quota Attainment," 2020.

It's our experience that the legacy approaches to professional selling are inadequate for addressing the complexity of the sales cycle. They don't provide enough help in guiding the client in a conversation that is nonlinear.

- Selling to existing clients provides a 60 to 70 percent chance of success. Selling to new prospects has a success rate of 5 to 20 percent.[9]

What we have recognized is that when prospective clients are provided an experience that doesn't create value for them, they disengage and refuse to commit to future meetings.

Which trend is having the biggest impact on your results and what are you noticing?

An Explanation of this Approach

My theory is that the leader of the sales force I am meeting with is already experiencing the challenges that virtually every sales organization is now facing. Instead of asking the decision-maker to share their problems and challenges with me, I started by explaining to them why they have those problems in the first place. You might also have noticed that I didn't try to create any credibility by pointing to my company.

The data I am providing is from third parties, parties with credibility and who stand to gain nothing from the client's decision to buy from me, eliminating the appearance of bias. Notice that I am using the One-Up strategy of explaining the implications of these trends and factors, inserting ideas about how best

---

[9] Taylor Landis, "Customer Retention Marketing vs. Customer Acquisition Marketing," OutboundEngine, April 20, 2021.

to address them—without ever mentioning that I have a solution. For example, I mention Year Zero, something that is not a product or a service or a solution. It's a concept the client could adopt to capture mindshare and engage with clients earlier in the buyer's journey.

When you start a conversation from the One-Up position, you will find that your clients mostly want to understand. They'll interrupt you with questions, and they will often share examples of how what you are sharing is already causing them problems. Don't bother asking your client what's keeping them up at night. Instead, seek to teach them what should be keeping them up at night or, better yet, explain why even the strongest chamomile tea can't overcome the mind-blowingly rapid changes in their environment. Later, when we look at how to help our clients change, you'll know to start by addressing the root cause of their problems, not just their temporary insomnia.

3

Insights and Information Disparity

Information is the resolution of uncertainty.

—*Claude Shannon*

YOU CANNOT BE One-Up without maintaining information disparity, which means you possess information your client is not aware of or has not yet recognized. The way you improve your client's decisions and results is by transferring your insights to them, moving them from One-Down to One-Up in the course of one or more conversations. This core strategy is the execution of "I know something you don't know. May I share it with you?"

Trade Secrets

When large companies started to professionalize sales in the 1920s, they had the advantage of total information disparity. Very little product information was easily available to prospects; Google was generations away, so outside of catalogs and stores, there was no way to learn about the increasing number of products and services ushered in by the Industrial Age. Both B2C and B2B customers had no choice but to speak with a salesperson. But those salespeople also had to gain the client's trust in their company, which they usually did by talking about the company's history or reputation. Not knowing who you could trust was an obstacle to buying and selling, especially with snake oil salesmen around every corner, so the rule of the day was *caveat emptor* (buyer beware).

Because information was scarce, the salesperson would also have to explain their product's features and benefits, using the opportunity to insist that the customer's friends and neighbors would be jealous of their shiny new SnarfBlat 3000. A salesperson with the power of information disparity could use it to take advantage of their prospective clients, not just by manipulating their egos but by withholding information or exaggerating their claims. For many customers, there was little recourse and no significant way for the customer to share complaints with a wide audience. The negative stereotype of the untrustworthy sales-man, one that has plagued the profession of sales for decades, took root in this environment.

Consider, for example, this talk track from General Motors' manual *Selling Chevrolets: A Book of General Information for Chevrolet Retail Salesmen*, published circa 1926. It appears in *Birth of a Salesman: The Transformation of Selling in America*, by Walter A. Friedman.

> Prospect: "My old car is worth at least $100.00 more than you offer me."
>
> Salesman: "Your old car, Mr. Prospect, has given you a lot of pleasure and service. You are thoroughly familiar with its condition, and I can understand how it may appear to you to be worth more. But the price of a used car, just like anything else, is determined by the demand for it. It is impossible to offer you more for your old car, much as we would like to do so, but we can offer you many quality features that cannot be duplicated in any other car at or near the price of a new Chev-rolet." (Show him features and ask for the order—often.)

In this example, the rather dismissive and somewhat con-descending salesperson is taught to exploit an information dis-parity about the market price and demand for used cars. There was little chance that the prospect would know whether the salesperson was taking advantage of them, a fact the salesperson could manipulate by unethically withholding certain informa-tion. General Motors didn't invent this bad behavior, but they did take full advantage of their customers' One-Down ignorance.

Today, however, using that technique would be impossi-ble. The prospect would say something like, "My car is worth $1,200 more than you are offering me, and even that is below Blue Book. In fact, your dealership just sold the same make and model with much higher mileage for $2,100 more than you are offering for mine." This relative information parity levels the playing field—and for particularly well-informed buyers, *caveat venditor* (seller beware) is the new rule.

The New Information Disparity

This drastic shift in information parity has rendered legacy approaches impotent. Remember that legacy approaches tend to start with easily available product information, which means they create no real value for the client. Likewise, while company reputation still plays a role, focusing on your company's history is almost never relevant to your prospect.

Here's the good news: While buyers can learn a lot from their own self-directed research, perhaps enough to make an expert consumer purchase, in a complex B2B sale, insight and experience are still necessary to good decision-making. Relying on your own knowledge for a complex purchase is like diagnosing yourself on WebMD: You might get a lot of information, but without the professional wisdom to apply it, you're likely to decide you have MacGregor's Syndrome. While there is substantial information parity when it comes to easily searchable facts, there is still an enormous information disparity; as John Cougar Mellencamp wrote, "I know a lot of things, but I don't know a lot of other things." As it turns out, your incredibly smart doctor can know less than your Sherpa about altitude sickness, especially when you doctor lives 500 feet above sea level.

To help move your B2B clients from One-Down to One-Up, you need to engage the new information disparity. Being One-Up requires you to correct that disparity in the areas where your clients are lacking insights, recommendations, and a prescription. In the past, salespeople used information disparity to take advantage of their customers; today, we create a parity of information that generates an advantage for our clients—all while helping us earn the right to their business.

You Don't Know What You Don't Know

One of the more helpful steps to improve your ability to be One-Up is to recognize that you are mostly One-Down. It's an act of intellectual humility to recognize that, regardless of your education, you are mostly ignorant. Personally, I try to become slightly less ignorant each day, knowing that no matter how much I learn, I still don't know what I don't know. You and your clients suffer that same human malady, because we'll never quite rid ourselves of information disparity.

It's difficult to know what is good and right and true in a world overrun by data and information, especially when sleek production quality can make poor ideas, incomplete information, and flat-out lies look like insight. You need look no further than opinions about your diet. Should you be following a ketogenic diet or eating raw foods? Is it better to be a carnivore, an omnivore, or a vegan? Should you practice intermittent fasting or eat three meals a day? More information often confuses people, and algorithms designed to keep your attention bring you more of what keeps you glued to your screens, the kind of pattern that causes people to believe that the earth is flat (or that a lower price is a better value).

One of the ways to determine which information to share is to ask what value it provides your contact. Information about your company or your products does not enable your client to do anything they could not already do, making that level of information a commodity, at best, if not outright meaningless. Using information disparity to your advantage means finding the areas where your insights and experiences let you enable your clients to solve a very different, and a more difficult, set of problems.

The New Information Disparity in Six Questions

The following six questions provide a way to think about where your contacts are missing information and how that causes them uncertainty—an idea contained in this chapter's epigraph from

Claude Shannon, the father of information theory. They're not exhaustive, but they're a good start.

What Is Going On?

The stakeholders you call on are head down, running their own business. Each day, they are confronted with new problems to go with an already large number of unresolved issues and challenges. Sure, they'd like to keep up with the trends, forces, and new innovations that would improve their decisions, but few have the time or bandwidth to do so. Peter Drucker, the greatest management thinker of all time, warned executives that the larger they grew their businesses, the more difficult it would be to create value for their clients, as their focus would naturally shift inward. Drucker himself had no staff, other than a typist to turn his handwritten pages into 53 books. His prediction was accurate for many sales organizations, where internal problems grow, leaving less attention for external value creation.

By creating a deficit of time and attention, the always-on modern workplace creates a new type of information disparity, but also gives you the opportunity to be One-Up, sharing information with your clients that will prevent them from being One-Down. When you can step in and give a client a briefing that catches them up on what is going on their world and how it impacts them, you are moving them closer to One-Up. Soon, they'll count on your briefings to keep them on top of their game, even requesting that you brief their teams and their bosses. They'll no longer have to worry about keeping up with what's going on, releasing that responsibility to you.

Why Am I Struggling to Produce Results?

Your clients have a deep need to discover what they don't know. This is something that is overlooked in legacy approaches, which base the entire discovery stage on unearthing a client's problem. Your clients already know they have a problem. In fact, they know they have a lot of problems, some more important than others, and a few they believe to be intractable. Here there should be parity, with both you and your client understanding the problems they are experiencing.

Much of the time, information disparity exists because your client does not understand what has changed outside of their company. The root causes of many of their problems are often trends and forces that your contacts aren't aware of (and may never recognize unless you share them). Eliminating that disparity not only helps your client but is all but certain to create a preference to work with—and buy from—you. Your ability to explain the implications of the external trends, factors, and forces preventing your clients from generating results begins to connect the dots for them. As we'll explore later in this chapter, the best way to solve your client's presenting problem is to deal with its root cause—and the best way to compel change is to show how the outside world drives those root causes.

What Am I Missing?

One question salespeople often ask is whether to tempt a prospective client by implying that they're working with the client's direct competitor. While this technically does correct a form of information disparity, it's a terrible strategy because it broadcasts that you cannot be trusted—a death knell for One-Upness. More importantly, there is a better way to use your knowledge and your experience to help your clients with the better results they need.

You would be better off saying something like, "We have learned a lot about your industry over the last eighteen months." This approach makes two notable gains: it piques your contact's curiosity, and it shows that you know things that your contact will find valuable. Decision-makers often fail to make decisions because they are missing information, so the people you serve want to know what they're missing. Some of that information comes from what other companies are doing and how well it's working. Because you work with dozens, hundreds, or thousands of clients, you have "situational knowledge," a form of experience that allows you to counsel your clients on what you see working, what you see failing to produce results, and the different factors that support or impede results.

Earlier in this chapter, you learned that you don't know what you don't know. It's often true that you also don't know what you *do* know until you're prompted to explain something to your client. The part of you that recognizes that something will or won't work for a specific client is a type of knowledge that is next to impossible for your client to match because they lack your experience. Catching them up means correcting their lack of information.

What Should I Do Now?

In my experience, there are three types of salespeople. The One-Up salesperson has recognized that they have information unknown to their client that comes from their experience, so they work to facilitate a needs-based, buyer's journey. The One-Down salesperson either does not have the experience to be One-Up or does not act on their One-Upness. The third type of salesperson is an order-taker, offering no information that would help the client improve anything.

A person considering a difficult decision will benefit from the guidance of someone who has helped other people enough, over time, to know best what they need to do. You, being One-Up as it pertains to this decision, are required to recommend what the client needs to do to successfully improve their position. You can only be consultative if you provide counsel, something the One-Up salesperson will have little trouble doing.

The One-Down salesperson that lacks experience may need help to know what to tell the client to do. The Order-Taker is of no use to their client.

There is no reason for prospects to buy from a person who cannot tell them what they need to do now, as that salesperson has not corrected their information disparity. The most valuable recommendation is not "buy our solution," but "here's how you should approach this decision." Helping your client understand what they need to do increases their preference to buy from you.

How Should I Change?

Your vantage point is a form of information disparity, one increasingly critical to creating and pursuing an opportunity with your client. Some companies use professional buyers and processes designed to position them as One-Up, as if their experience buying something occasionally is a match for the insights of a One-Up salesperson who helps different companies with that same decision every day. That mismatch can cause your client significant problems.

John Kotter, a scholar at Harvard Business School, provides an eight-step framework for change in *The Heart of Change: Real-Life Stories of How People Change Their Organizations*. The eight steps are increase urgency, build the guiding team, get the vision right, communicate for buy-in, empower action, create short-term wins, don't let up, and make change stick. Imagine your client has met with four different salespeople, each of whom has asked the client about their "problem," then immediately tried to sell them a "solution." The client, however, has not done anything about their problem. What prevents a person or a group of people from making change is a complicated mix of factors, most of which come from lacking information, alignment, or the ability to build consensus.

Starting our conversations by showing how external forces and trends are the root cause of the client's problems is one way to help increase their sense of urgency (more on that in Chapter 9). The reason we provide our client our One-Up vantage point is so we can help them build that guiding team earlier in the process. While Kotter's third step has the guiding team developing the vision, that vision will benefit from you guiding the guiding team. The reason salespeople lose deals or watch them stall is often because they don't understand how to help their clients change. The One-Down salesperson doesn't believe it is their role to tell the client what they need to do (something that makes them anti-consultative).

How Can I Be Certain of Success?

There is never a reason to lie to your clients. The reason some clients believe all salespeople lie to them is that many salespeople lie by omission, an age-old problem built on information disparity. In a large sales call with my team, a senior leader expressed concern about our ability to produce the results he needed. My team was stunned when I replied, "We normally get things right on the fourth or fifth try. There is always a steep learning curve in projects like this." The senior leader looked at me, smiled, and said, "How good are you guys? It takes us at least eleven or twelve tries." We both knew I was telling the truth.

One way to stay One-Down is to stay quiet about the problems and challenges you and your client are sure to encounter in any significant change initiative. In fact, addressing those challenges helps create a sense of certainty for your client. The fact that you know what is likely to go wrong means you know how to avoid it, and how to deal with it should it crop up anyway. To lie about the challenges that come with change is to be perpetually One-Down, due to your fear of losing.

One of the reasons clients don't buy from salespeople is because they lack the certainty that they can succeed. By showing your stakeholders the steps you will take together, especially in a written and illustrated form, you provide a sense of certainty that discourages them from crawling back to the cold comfort of the status quo. Your experience shows you the common concerns your clients may have, providing you the opportunity to address their uncertainty by sharing your plan to ensure their success.

The Value of Being One-Up and Information Disparity

As I've said before, one reason I am critical of the legacy approaches to sales is that they advise salespeople against doing any "free consulting." This is an attempt to maintain information disparity unless and until your client buys your product. This approach puts a salesperson in a deep One-Down position, one in which they are afraid that their prospect is going to steal their idea and share it with other salespeople, who in turn will pass it off as their own. Occasionally that does happen, but keep a couple of things in mind. First, any competitor desperate enough to steal your idea clearly doesn't have any better ideas of their own. Second, they almost certainly don't know how to execute the idea. You may want to help the client by exposing their poor decision-making, gently reminding them that they were—and still are—One Down:

> I am concerned about your future results. If the partner you chose was not already aware of this strategy, it's certain they have no experience and no idea about the four risks that you are taking or how to address each one. Make sure you have them explain those risks before you let them start. Also make sure they explain the two follow-up projects you're going to need to maximize your results. Depending on what happens or how bad it is, we may or may not be able to help you. Why would you try something like this with anyone who hasn't already done it, and what are people going to think when the train comes off the tracks?

Being One-Up allows you to use information disparity in a more powerful and more ethical way, one that serves the client by helping them change. The approach of being One-Up leaves no room for fear of your client stealing your "free consulting." After all, we live in a dynamic time, so what works today will be a nonstarter tomorrow (or perhaps the day after, but not much further into the future than that). You are not going to run out of ideas and insights because the world is going to continue to provide disruptive events, new trends, and forces that are going to require you and your clients to change.

More practically, the One-Up approach saves you from showing up and giving your client the same conversation they have had with every salesbot, er, salesperson who ever booked a meeting with them. Salespeople often complain about not wanting to be treated like a commodity, only to provide a conversation that has been irredeemably commoditized. The problem-pain-solution approach has lost its efficacy and is being replaced by newer, more effective strategies and tactics. By being One-Up, you create value beyond your solution. The value you create supports change management, enables well-informed decisions, and provides the advice and recommendations that lead to better results. That's what makes up a truly consultative sales approach.

Learning from Yourself

In Chapter 7, we are going to take a deeper dive into building your external insights, focusing on sources outside your company and your experience. But you should also recognize the many internal insights you already possess; they come from your training and experience.

Maintaining your One-Upness is both your obligation and your best tool for professional development. It's important that your clients can count on you to know the things they need to know, making you a source of knowledge and insights. Without a commitment to maintaining that information disparity, you risk being a one-hit wonder. You might dazzle your client with insights in your first meeting, but if you can't consistently repeat your performance, they'll look to some other motivated knows-quite-a-lot to step into your role. There are several areas you can explore to keep your insights fresh and relevant to your clients' decisions and results, so you always have something new and useful to share.

- **Inside Your Four Walls.** Before you go searching outside your four walls, start by recognizing what you—and, perhaps, your One-Up team members—have learned through your individual and collective experience. You want to start by documenting what your experience already provides in the way of useful insights.
- **The Value of Your Client's Experiences and Challenges.** Every day, you interact with clients and prospective clients. Your conversations provide you with insights that can be helpful to both parties if you are willing to recognize and capture them. For example, when your clients explain the new challenges confronting their business, it's a good bet that other companies in their industry are either already feeling those same challenges or soon will be. What you learn working with one client is almost certain to be useful to another.

  Here is a prompt to help you get started: What did you learn working with your clients over the last twelve months? A list of "ten things we learned last year" will provide enough insight to use in an executive briefing or as a conversation starter. Your experience is only useful if you share the lessons, and it is sometimes as powerful as data.
- **What's Working, What's Not, and Why.** Because you and your peers (hopefully, a bunch of fellow One-Up sales folks) are working to help your clients improve their results, you get to experience what works and why. The "why" here is

incredibly important, because it helps you to understand where and when one approach might be the best choice. Improving your clients' results is not a one-size-fits-all process. Here's a brainstorming prompt: What works for one client but fails for another, and what factors seem to explain the difference?

- **Your Experience of What Is Necessary to Produce Results.** Chapter 11 (in this book, not the bankruptcy law) is about helping your client change, going well beyond picking a new supplier and a new "solution." Your ability to be truly consultative means knowing exactly what your client needs to change to be able to produce the better results they need. Believing that this isn't your responsibility will demote you to the One-Down position.

  Start by asking this: What do your clients need to change to improve their results, or what do they do that prevents them from being able to generate better outcomes?

- **How to Make Change.** In Chapter 6, we'll look more deeply into "buying insights," the conversations your clients will need to commit to having to successfully transform their results. One obstacle to solving your client's problems is a poor approach to making changes at all. You can start to organize your "change-related" information and insights by recognizing the conversations your clients skip and the commitments they would prefer not to make or keep.

As One-Up sales professionals, the reason we maintain information disparity is to continually refresh our insights, so we can share our ideas, knowledge, and experience to help all our clients improve their futures.

4

Supporting Client Discovery

He not busy being born is busy dying.

—Bob Dylan

ONE OF THE responsibilities of being One-Up is occasionally disputing your client's beliefs and questioning the way they do things. Some salespeople consider that approach rude or even heretical, mainly because it challenges what they believe about sales and professionalism. But you are only a heretic when you are early to recognize a new insight or practice. Later, you will be called prescient, a trailblazer, or a groundbreaker.

In the movie *The Matrix*, Neo was acutely aware that he was One-Down. He recognized that the mysterious character called Morpheus was One-Up and was his key to understanding reality. Sensing he was missing something, Neo worked to correct his One-Downness. Morpheus offered to show him what he wanted to see by offering Neo the choice of two pills (lenses). The red pill would let him see reality, while the blue pill would let him fall back into the warm, comfortable sleep that he had known all his life. Reading past this line means you are taking the red pill and all that it reveals, even if it may disturb your long-held beliefs.

What if I told you that the most powerful discovery strategy is not asking questions to identify your client's problems and pain, but instead helping them discover something about themselves? What if you were responsible for teaching your clients something that would enable them to improve their decision-making and their future? What if there were more to discovery than a commoditized call that your client must suffer through, even though it offers no novelty and no return on their precious time?

Why "Best Practices" Fail

In *Eat Their Lunch*, a book about stealing clients away from your competition, I introduce a framework called Level 4 Value Creation. The idea is both simple and transformational. The first level of value is your product or service, both of which are already commodities. The second level of value is your company's experience, shaping the service and support you provide your clients—useful, but ultimately just table stakes, creating nothing powerful enough to compel decision-makers to change. The third level of value is solving the client's problem, something that the legacy solution approaches sought to address. The fourth level of value is enabling the strategic outcomes the client needs, going well beyond their presenting problem. While legacy discovery started with Level 1 and made its way through the highly commoditized parts of the value stack, modern discovery reverses that order, beginning with a conversation about your client's strategic outcomes.

There is a certain point when a "best practice" is overused to the point that it can no longer be considered a best practice. David Snowden, a management consultant, would tell you that best practices can backfire when dealing with complexity. Certain inflection points reduce or eliminate the value of what was once the standard way of doing things. We have reached this point in professional sales, as decision-makers face different sets of problems, something we can think of as *the problems that prevent them from solving their problems*. Often, a client will enter the sales process because they are trying to solve a particular problem. They don't need a salesperson to "discover" something they already know. However, there are almost always other problems the client isn't aware of, and those unrecognized issues can prevent them from being successful. The new discovery process is about analyzing a complex situation so your clients can learn something about themselves.

In that spirit, please allow me to help you discover something about yourself and your approach to the discovery call.

Before we look at a One-Up discovery call, let's imagine a typical legacy presentation: Salesperson A walks into a client's office, desperately attempts to create rapport, spits out a bunch of facts about his company, points to his high-profile clients, and hopes his contact finds him credible. He then asks the client a set of questions designed get them to confess that they have a problem. Salesperson A is not overly concerned about the client's experience. He just wants to present his solution as the answer to the client's problem, the analgesic that will dull their pain. Salesperson A believes selling this "solution" is only possible through a straight-line path: problem, pain, solution. That said, he is personable, polite, and professional, even if the conversation isn't compelling enough to keep the client from continually looking at their watch.

Two days later, Salesperson B sits down in the very same chair in the very same conference room. Within the first three minutes, the prospective client gets a dreadful sense of déjà vu. You guessed it: Salesperson B executes the same approach as his competitor, working his way to the client's pain point. In fact, the conversations are so alike that the client finds it nearly impossible to tell the two salespeople apart. Perhaps Salesperson A was a bit taller, while Salesperson B used a green logo—yes, that must have been it, because the client's childhood rumpus room had a carpet nearly the same shade. Nothing else stood out about their expertise, solutions, or suitability as a strategic partner.

Here is more evidence of commoditization: Not only does your client know their lines, but they also know your lines and the timing of each scene. They've been so well-rehearsed over the years that many could walk through their side of the conversation without you offering them a single prompt. The more salespeople your contacts have met with, the more they know what's coming. You cannot expect to differentiate yourself when your client has already seen your act because your competitor did it in Tuesday's matinee show.

A Well-Worn Pattern

The structure of the legacy sales conversation was sound in its time, but like everything else, it must evolve to address the new business environment. There has been too little novelty for too long, and the former "best practices" no longer create the level of value our clients need.

The sequence of conversations is just as big a problem as their content. Here is the order in which sales conversations are conducted in legacy approaches to B2B sales:

1. **Rapport-Building.** The idea here is that small talk at the beginning of the conversation helps the salesperson connect with their prospective client, making them more likely to buy from them. The conversation might include the weather, the local sports team's performance, the news of the day, or more personal things like the client's children or something that they might have in common. While it's important to be known, liked, and trusted, it's more important that you don't position yourself as a time-waster.

2. **Our Company.** This approach is over one hundred years old. Starting a conversation with your company as the subject is designed to do two things: prove that your client can trust the company, and provide the salesperson with credibility. This approach is favored by most marketers, because they believe the company's story is important to share early on. Unfortunately, this approach immediately identifies you and what you sell as a commodity.

3. **Our Clients.** This is the B2B equivalent of social proof. A slide with your client's logos was designed to impress your client and position your company as successful, competent, and trustworthy. If the largest companies in the world trust your company, it must be a safe choice. But if you make it this far in your slide deck without doing anything to prove your relevance, you are rapidly losing credibility by having nothing to say.

4. **Our Solutions.** Having established that your company is a perfect fit for the prospective client, the next step is to inform

your prospective client about your products or services. Many still practice this approach, believing it somehow helps gain the client's trust. The client who was hoping you were somehow interested in helping them improve their results feels the sharp pain of having to sit through yet another "why us" conversation, a pernicious sort of torture that hasn't yet been banned by the Geneva Convention. When that conversation does not include the solution, the salesperson anxiously skips straight to identifying the client's problem and their pain by asking questions.

5. **Discover a Problem.** In the legacy solution approach, the primary function of the sales call is to identify or elicit a problem, find the pain, and then solve the problem by recommending their solution. This phase might also include a conversation to make sure the solution fits the client's problem.

Many salespeople, especially those with empathy and experience, have started to skip straight to discovering a problem—they recognize, at least, that the old lead-up creates no value for the client and steals time that would be better spent trying to serve the client, even if it's only marginally better than asking about the client's pain points. An honest assessment of the state of the discovery call would reveal that salespeople have executed the same approach for so long that they are simply going through the motions, especially when both players know their parts by rote.

A Modern Discovery Call

The day before I started writing this chapter, a client asked me to meet with them, telling me their team wanted a "dog-and-pony show." When I arrived, the client's team briefed me for twenty minutes with a slide deck that had their marketing team's fingerprints all over it. They wanted me to know who they were. The minute they finished their briefing, the senior leader ignored the entire slide deck and instead asked me a single question. They wanted to understand their world, why they were struggling, and how best to approach a new initiative. I answered with the content of an executive briefing, rattling off the data and explaining why they were struggling. Why would you spend time on something that you know creates too little value for the people you are trying to help, when you could offer so much more by changing what you include in discovery calls?

This sequence of a modern discovery call is certainly different and may seem uncomfortable at first. That's because it changes the main question from "why us" to "why change," making your client the focus of the conversation. It goes something like this:

1. **Executive Briefing.** Starting with a conversation that explains your client's world helps them understand the forces behind many of their current (or near-future) problems. For decades, the commoditized sales call has sought to identify pain points, but it is certain that your clients already know they have problems. You also want to be certain that you have a good idea of their challenges, since you help other clients with them as your full-time profession. This is part of what makes you a sense maker.

2. **Exploration of Change.** Because you already know what problems your client is likely to be experiencing, you can move to a more robust conversation about what changes they must make to improve their results. The best way to do this is through a series of questions designed to help your client discover something about themselves, something we'll have more to say about later in this chapter.

3. **The Pivot.** From the conversation about the forces impacting your client's results, you can pivot by asking for a meeting to share some of what you have learned about improving results, by sharing what you see working and not working in your client's market and industry.

4. **Rapport Building.** After creating value for your client in any meeting, you can work on a personal relationship. Most salespeople either overestimate the value of rapport, believing a personal relationship is the key to winning, or underestimate it, believing "fit" is not important to long-term relationships. It can be tricky to find that balance; just be sure not to overstay your welcome.

It's important to recognize that different places have different customs when it comes to these kinds of conversations, so you should tailor your approach based on what you know—and learn—about the client. For example, in the Northeast Corridor of the United States, say from Washington, D.C., to Connecticut, businesspeople tend to value efficiency over personal connections, so rapport-building at the beginning of a call may be a mistake. Conversely, in the South and some parts of the Midwest, you'll be seen as rude if you don't take the time to talk about your people, where you're from, and who you know. Do what you know to be right based on how things work where you sell, even if it means adjusting the structure of your discovery conversations.

Above all, give your clients and prospective clients an interesting experience. Christopher Hitchens, whose likeness adorns a wall in my office, suggested that "the one unforgivable sin is to be boring." For now, I will forgive you, even if your prospective clients won't.

Checking the Boxes on Dissatisfaction

There are areas where you are One-Up and your client is One-Down. Neither searching for a problem nor articulating the gap between their current results and the future results they need is likely to create a lot of value for the people you call on. You don't want to be the thirty-third or thirty-fourth salesperson to ask them some version of "What's keeping you up at night?" nor do you want to be fourteenth to ask, "What do you wish your existing supplier did better?" These questions must feel like a recurring nightmare to the client and are an affront to professional selling.

It's easy to unwittingly commoditize yourself. If you look and sound like every other salesperson who darkens your dream client's door, they can't recognize any distinction—even one that might actually make a difference. You can ask the same questions that every other salesperson asks in discovery, replaying the not-so-greatest hits of the conversations your prospective client has had multiple times with a plethora of peddlers, all of whom are completely One-Down. You can present your company and your solution as the right choice, but chances are your client will know the ending long before you get to the punch line.

Once, I created a list of all the reasons that might cause a client to change, giving copies to all the salespeople on my team so they could keep track of our clients' problems. One client ended up sitting on the same side of the table as the salesperson, and after spotting the checklist, he picked it up and promptly checked off all the boxes that applied to his company, as calmly as if he were just ordering sushi. He handed it back to the salesperson, who was not certain what to do. If your only reason to do discovery is to identify a problem, find the pain, and pitch your solution, then you may as well offer your client a menu of problems and ask them if they want fries with that.

You may not have recognized that your attempt to differentiate your company and your solution results in a commoditized client experience, making it more difficult to find anything that would cause someone to choose you over one of your many competitors. But the more you behave like a commodity, the more you'll be treated like one. The only way to break free from that perception is to provide a different and better client experience.

Occupying the One-Up position flips traditional discovery on its head. Instead of asking your client, "What's keeping you up at night?" you tell them, "These are the things that are or soon will be keeping you up at night." When you can explain why your client is experiencing their challenges, you are not going to sound or feel like Salesperson A or Salesperson B. Instead, you will be radically different in a way that truly has an impact. When you are able to recognize the problems that prevent your contacts from solving their real, complex problems, you are moving toward One-Up.

It is impossible not to know what challenges your prospective clients are facing when you've been helping others deal with those same problems. Those experiences are etched on your mind, allowing you to see the repeating pattern of problems, challenges, and opportunities, often minutes after your client starts speaking. You don't have to read your client's mind to know where and why they need help. You see the patterns every day.

Why would you start the most crucial conversation to creating value with no idea or theory of what should cause your prospective clients to change? And why would you ask a prospective client for a meeting without a strong belief that you could help them improve some specific result? Spending time trying to find a problem that a prospective client will admit to subtracts from value. I'm confident that you already know what your client's problem is, simply because you have already helped dozens or hundreds of clients engage similar challenges. Those clients bought from you because they needed your help to solve their problem or eliminate something that was harming their results. One way you might start developing your theories is to create a table that shows the problem, the root cause, and the implications for your prospective clients. That's enough to have a working hypothesis.

The Aha Moment and Insight Transfer

If you can, recall a discovery call where you asked your client a question that caused them to blurt out, "That's a great question."

Your client's response is proof positive you are One-Up and that you have just created the possibility of moving them from One-Down to One-Up. Your question taught them something about themselves, their world, or an idea that will help them make a better decision in the future. Write down the question, too, if you remember it. In fact, you always want to write down good language, no matter when or where you find it. The best salespeople have the best language, and you should steal from them without shame, knowing they stole it from another salesperson. Over time, you will create novel language choices, and when I hear you say them, know that they may well become part of my repertoire.

The value of an insight-based approach to sales lies in creating the aha moments where your clients discover something about themselves. Those moments allow your contacts to recognize a new perspective, new potential, and new choices. These are prerequisites to change.

18 Things You Can Help Your Clients Discover

1. **Their Assumptions Are Outdated.** One of the primary ways you correct your client is replacing their false or outdated assumptions. An insight-based approach allows you to replace those assumptions, updating them to current reality.
2. **The Nature of Their Mistakes.** Your clients don't set out to make mistakes when making decisions. Much of the time, the mistakes are the result of their being One-Down but still buying from a One-Down salesperson from a One-Down sales organization. You can help them learn something about themselves by providing the insights and information that enables better future decisions.
3. **The Conversations They Need to Have to Move Forward.** Your vantage point provides your decision-makers and decision-shapers with a view of the sales conversation that

improves their future results by ensuring they have certain crucial conversations.

4. **Who Needs to Participate in a Change Initiative.** You can help your client pursue the change they need by ensuring they build consensus, bring the right people into the conversation to ensure they can successfully decide for their business, and craft the cohesion necessary to execute their new initiative.

5. **What Has Changed and Why.** When you teach your clients what has changed and why, you are teaching them something about themselves, namely how they need to change to be able to succeed in their environment.

6. **The Better Results Available to Them.** One of the reasons some companies are not producing better results is that they don't know those results are possible. When you show them that better results are available to them, you not only teach them something about themselves but also compel them to change.

7. **The Obstacles to Improving Their Results.** Everyone claims to want better results, but sometimes your clients need you to directly point out the obstacles they are going to need to address to be able to improve their results. Most One-Down reps would prefer not to make these known.

8. **The Forces That Will Impact Their Business.** You will find that insights about the forces that will impact your client's business do a good deal of work, helping them discover where they are in space and how to prepare or respond to those forces.

9. **New Opportunities Available to Them.** Most of the time, your clients are head down, doing their work. Because they are not looking up to see what's changed, there are often new opportunities available to them that they have not yet recognized. Help them discover these opportunities by sharing them with your contacts.

10. **The Potential Negative Outcomes of the Status Quo.** The status quo is increasingly dangerous in a complex environment. The longer a client goes without changing, the more certain it is that they are falling behind, something you need to help them discover through the sales conversation.

11. **What to Start Doing Now to Improve Their Results.** In a later chapter, you will learn that some of the most important advice and recommendations have little or nothing to do with your company, your product, or your service. You can help your client discover what they need to do to improve their results.

12. **What to Stop Doing Now to Improve Their Results.** Occasionally, your client will need your help to discover what they need to stop doing. I once had a company cold call me to tell me to stop doing something—and following their advice ended up massively improving my results.

13. **What Should Be Compelling Change.** This is a big one, and you will recognize that it is a large part of both this book and the One-Up approach. What makes you a good strategic partner is being proactive, especially when your guidance prevents your client from harm by helping them change before they are forced to.

14. **How to Evaluate Different Approaches.** In a later chapter on triangulation strategy, you will learn how to help your clients evaluate their choices of partners and their strategies to deliver value, including the concessions your clients don't know they've agreed to until they harm their results.

15. **Insights That Are Unavailable to Them.** Some of your insights are not available to your contacts because they lack your experience. You can learn much by helping your clients improve their results, and all that you learn will help you help your client discover something about themselves.

16. **What Is Working for Other Companies.** Your client isn't able to go to other companies and ask them to tell them how

to improve their results. You, however, can be a deep well of insights about what is working for other companies.

17. **What Is Not Working and Why.** Sometimes things that once worked well are no longer effective. Your client may need to learn that their preferred methods are ineffective now. When you can explain why, you help them make a new discovery about their company and their need to change.

18. **How Best to Pursue Change.** Your client may want and need to change but not know how to go about pursuing the change they need. You can shed some light on what your client will need to do to take a run at a real change initiative.

Questions That Help Clients Discover

The very best tactic is to ask a question that causes the client to recognize that they are missing something—and by doing so, realize there are new choices available to them. For example, here's a question that might have helped you before you started reading this book: "We know that 59 percent of buyers don't want to meet with a salesperson because they don't believe the salesperson is helping them with their agenda; instead they are just pushing their solution. What are the core changes that you have made to create greater value in the sales conversation, if any, and have you started to consider any new strategies?"

Before you started your journey to One-Up, you may not yet have recognized that the primary vehicle you have for creating value, differentiating yourself, and winning clients is the sales conversation. If you had not made any changes to your sales approach, you might have recognized a gap. By this point, I hope you have a significant list of improvements.

Before we look at a few additional examples, remember to ask questions that are artful and effective. In the question above, if I had left off the phrases "if any" and "have you started to consider any new strategies," you might have been suspicious about my intentions or even gotten upset at the question. Being One-Up does not mean that you make your client feel as if they are One-Down. Good language is designed to assuage the client's ego-driven need to defend themselves from you and your challenging questions. (In Chapter 11, you'll find a direct and candid approach that is sometimes necessary to move your client to change, but that comes later.)

Here are some more sample questions that apply the same principles.

- *"In the past six months, have you started any new initiatives around this key result, and have you started conversations about what changes you might need to pursue over the next twelve months? If you haven't, can I share a couple things we see working?"* This question provides a view that suggests action is necessary, and that your client should have started sooner, without convicting them of negligence.
- *"How prepared is your team to address these challenges and what level would you say they are at when it comes to the readiness to change?"* This is a buyer insight question that teaches the client to consider where their team is when it comes to change and points to consensus.
- *"Is it better to change on your timeline? What challenges would you have if you were forced to do it on a timeline that isn't of your choosing?"* This is a value-based question that shows the client the potential negative consequences.
- *"Your experience is not uncommon because some people won't tell you about the concessions you are agreeing to when you choose their lowest-price delivery model. What was it that caused you to recognize that things were not working the way you expected?"* This is a more difficult question that reveals a truth, but you have to use it carefully and with the utmost skill. Here, you might have to look closely at what the client is discovering

about themselves. The client has learned that lower-priced offerings come with concessions that no one shares with them before they buy.

You'll find the strategy behind attacking your competitor's models in Chapter 10 on triangulation strategy, one of the core methods for helping your client improve their decision-making and their results. You can help your client discover something about themselves without harming the relationship. In this case, you're helping the client discover that the lowest price does not often come with a lower cost; these two concepts may be at odds. It also helps them recognize that they made concessions that were never disclosed to them, something that will cause them to ask more and better questions in the future. This is a bit heavier and deeper than what we covered earlier. But professional selling requires you to see something that is invisible to most.

How to Help Your Client Discover

We've established that the traditional problem-pain-solution pattern of a discovery call has now been completely commoditized. Anything that is commoditized lacks the value creation that might differentiate it. For you to help your clients with self-discovery, you are going to need to see things that are invisible to your client—and unavailable to your competitors. Some of these clues are delicate, but all of them have the potential to reveal something important to a client who is struggling.

Subjective Beliefs

Personally, I am not a big fan of reality. No one consulted me on my opinion as to how things should work in the universe or on the humble, little, out-of-the-way rock circling a giant ball of fire and occupied by some rather unpleasant characters. However, as far as I have been able to discern, reality isn't swayed by my opinion. It also doesn't concern itself with what your clients believe. Your clients may not love their reality, but they do have to accept it if they want better outcomes.

Some of your clients are going to hold beliefs and assumptions (anchors) that are in conflict with reality. One of my clients, for example, believed that labor was abundant and cheap. That subjective (and false) belief was an obstacle to the better results they needed.

People cling to their subjective beliefs. They try very hard to protect them from any attack that might suggest that they are not true. You need to be smart, well-researched, and in possession of all the diplomacy necessary to help your client see that their baby is not just ugly but downright hideous. Later, we'll talk about the types of questions you might ask and when to get permission to share. For this example, we will ask for permission: "Would it be okay if I shared with you some data and what we believe it means? It hasn't been widely shared but it does a good job of explaining what's changed over the last eighteen months. It might provide you with a distinct advantage right now."

Objective Evidence

Sometimes, your client will have evidence that facilitates an insight transfer. One of my clients shared with me that their top ten salespeople had over a 90 percent win rate. I was both impressed and more than a little skeptical; I told the client that if that number was accurate, he should try to get the number down to 40 percent by making them compete for deals that are more difficult to win. Instead, he reviewed the deals they had pursued and lost. On average, it turned out, they had just over a 10 percent win rate. The secret to their high win rates was not documenting their losses.

I would bet that a high percentage of salespeople never ask clients for any data that might allow them to apply their own insights, ultimately providing their client with a clearer view of their business and their results. At one business, I asked clients for financial information to show them that their spending was much higher than they believed. There are a lot of ways to ask for data, but here is an example: "Can you share with me these three metrics to analyze, so we can explore what you might want to prioritize to improve your results in this area?" Pro tip: Don't do anything that might cause your client to believe you are judging them or their results.

Conflicts of Culture and Consensus

One of the best things that can happen to you is for one of your dream client's decision-makers—the one who refuses to meet with you—to take a new job and be replaced by a new leader. Many new leaders are hard-chargers who want quick wins, especially early in their tenure. But because they are unaware of the culture of their new teams, they attempt to withdraw a larger amount of relationship capital than they can cover, depleting their account. The One-Up approach allows you to help your client understand that they need to build consensus to solve problems. You can help address this gap by asking a simple but challenging question: "Have you started the process of building consensus or building the guiding team who can help you bring their teams with them?"

Conflicts with the Environment

Changing environments often makes it easy for you to recognize a conflict that can illuminate your client's challenges and possibilities. Companies like Blockbuster did not recognize that the future was streaming. The taxi industry did not believe the future was an unmarked car, an app, and a better experience. The one thing you can count on is a universe that creates and destroys, only to create and destroy again. Your client needs a higher-resolution lens so they can see these challenges early enough and clearly enough to do something about them—before they become a problem. Here's one question you might ask: "Have you started to address the demographic shifts that are going to make it more expensive to acquire and take care of your clients?"

These questions provide you with a number of opportunities to help your client see something more clearly, allowing them to learn something about themselves. They are like lenses that allow you and your client to see things at a higher resolution. Looking through the lenses of objective evidence and truth allows you to discover how a client's assumptions, misconceptions, culture, and environment work together to create a complex problem. The next chapter is about how to multiply these lenses and refocus on the problem to develop a real solution.

5

Your Role as a Sense Maker

What is essential is invisible to the eye.

—Antoine de Saint-Exupéry

THE WORLD LOOKS very different when you view it through a new lens. During my life, I have sought out lenses that provide a clearer view of myself, other people, the world, and the nature of reality. Unfortunately, not everyone shares that goal. We live in a time of extreme polarization, one in which people refuse to acknowledge—let alone respect—other people's perspectives. One of the keys to personal and professional growth is to get outside yourself, so you can not only respect but also understand others' lenses. Let me give you a few examples of how other One-Up experts have helped me reach that goal.

In 1995, I was walking past the new nonfiction releases at Barnes & Noble when I noticed a book with a strange cover and a provocative title: *The Lucifer Principle: A Scientific Expedition into the Forces of History* by Howard Bloom. The book was a master class in memetics, showing how ideas compete. You might believe that you possess ideas, but ideas possess you. They're like viruses, infecting individuals and spreading. The strongest ones compete to prevent others from replacing them. If you are going to be infected by ideas, you should shop for those that are proven to improve your life and your results, rejecting the limiting beliefs that will constrain every area of your life. Influenced by Bloom's work (and our friendship), I will describe what I think of as a *higher-resolution lens*, one that provides a clearer view and more information.

A few years later, in 2001, I found a book by Nassim Nicholas Taleb with the title *Fooled by Randomness: The Hidden Role of Chance in Life and in the Markets*. Taleb is a professional trader, and this book was his first attempt to explain how and why we don't recognize randomness—and instead try to make sense of our world by constructing an explanation that would make everything nonrandom. His second book, *The Black Swan: The Impact of the*

Highly Improbable, provided an even clearer view of our foolhardy attempts to predict what cannot be predicted. His third book, *Antifragile: Things That Gain from Disorder*, provides a philosophy for not only avoiding harm from disorder but actually profiting from it. All three are well worth your time.

Later, in 2015, I found an article about Ken Wilber and integral theory, a model of cognition that includes all other lenses. The four quadrants into which Wilber fits the entire universe are Individual Exteriors, Individual Interiors, Collective Exteriors, and Collective Interiors. Inside those four quadrants we find lines, levels, states, and types. The most accessible way to acquire Wilber's lens is by listening to the audio program *Kosmic Consciousness*, a twelve-hour interview that allows you to recognize his sense of humor and the playfulness he brings to his work. A friend and mentor, Wilber taught me that even though some forces allow us to rise above our current level, there are as many or more forces trying to pull us (and our clients) down.

You and I see the world through a lens restricted by our limited knowledge, our limited experience, our limited understanding, and by all the ideas we have been infected with. Every individual perspective is influenced by cultural norms, including the norms in your clients' companies and industries. Your clients can only see what their existing lens provides them—including how they view their problems, challenges, and opportunities. To help your clients expand and sharpen their view, you have to provide them with a higher-resolution lens, one that enables better decisions and better results.

The Value of a Higher-Resolution Lens

Being One-Up requires that you provide your client with a higher-resolution lens. So far, you've refined that lens using your insights, your ability to correct your client's information disparity, and your ability to help them learn something about themselves. Executing these strategies and tactics will create a tremendous advantage for you, and it will do even more for your clients. It will also differentiate you from your competition in ways essentially immune to their outdated and One-Down legacy approaches.

Imagine your prospective client is looking through a telescope. The lens is a little foggy, so it is tough to get a clear view of the terrain in front of them. There is a medical condition called a scotoma, a blind spot in an otherwise normal visual field. That is what it's like when your clients look through their telescope; their view of their business, their problems, and their future is incomplete. To help them see what they need to move forward, you gently ask to borrow their telescope and fit it with a new lens, one that allows them to see clearly what was right in front of them. Without your higher-resolution lens, your contacts will decide while lacking the full picture, leading to less-than-optimal outcomes.

The reason decision-makers, decision-shapers, and buyers experience remorse is because they recognize after the fact that they made a wrong decision. This regret typically appears once they learn something that would have caused them to make a different decision, like the fact that their new method (or their refusal to change) fails to produce the better results they needed. A higher-resolution lens gives them the information they need to make the next strategic decision and it significantly reduces buyer's remorse.

Complexity, Confusion, and Paralysis

Part of the value of a higher-resolution lens is that it allows clients to appreciate the complexity of their business and environment. Scott Page, a complexity expert and professor at the University of Michigan, defines complexity this way: "When we describe something as complex, we mean that it consists of interdependent, diverse entities, and we assume that those entities adapt—that they respond to their local and global environments."[1] Human beings eventually adapt, but complexity often induces paralysis, an inability to respond appropriately to the environment. Assumptions and subjective beliefs give leaders a false sense of security, making them believe they have plenty of time to respond once an issue emerges. For example, leaders who believe their organizations are too big to fail may wait too long to respond to external forces.

Before 2007, the year that Apple CEO Steve Jobs announced the iPhone, Nokia and Blackberry dominated the cellular phone market. Uber started in 2010, but it was years before New York City taxis had an app. (The last person to buy a New York City taxi medallion for $1,000,000 made a terrible decision, not recognizing that it would soon be essentially worthless.)

A complex environment makes it difficult to know what to do and when to do it. When humans are uncertain, waiting can feel like the safe choice. The longer you have worked in sales, the more you'll see clients wait longer than they should to address the forces that eventually harm their business. But when you're One-Up, you can create the certainty to help your clients act before they are harmed.

One-Up Sense-Making: Opening Up the Aperture

I have a tough time with the negative stereotype of pushy, dishonest, and know-nothing salespeople, especially since it's persisted long after the most egregious behaviors have been all but abandoned in B2B and B2C sales. Still, many salespeople

---

[1] Scott Page, https://www.audible.com/pd/Understanding-Complexity-Audiobook/1629976849?ref=a_library_t_c5_libItem_&pf_rd_p=80765e81-b10a-4f33-b1d3-ffb87793d047&pf_rd_r=3ZDP38K168G8RR8PPB75.

today are guilty of a lack of value creation—that is, they waste their prospect's time by trying to solve their own problems first. In reality, the fates of a salesperson and their prospective client are tied together; the clients' problems become the salesperson's problems.

Grab a random salesperson out of crowd and ask them if they believe they are supposed to solve their clients' problems. That salesperson will vigorously nod their head in agreement, then tell you how they help their clients by selling them the solution to their problem. Add nine more salespeople to the survey and you'll get much the same response. But what you won't find is attention to a deeper set of problems, the ones that prevent the client from abandoning a harmful status quo before it harms them.

In Chapter 3, you learned that information disparity still exists, but the content has shifted. It's now easy for clients to find information about your company and your products, but much harder for your contacts to make sense of their world, pursue solutions to their problems, and help other stakeholders recognize the need to change so it creates alignment around what they should do. Providing a One-Up, higher-resolution lens is one way to balance the new information disparity.

The reason it is difficult for salespeople and their clients to solve the client's presenting problem—the one that's driven the client to seek help in the first place—is that a series of wicked problems—often unrecognized by the client—hold them back. What makes a problem wicked is that it resists resolution, especially when complex interdependencies and integral contradictions mean that efforts to solve one aspect may reveal or create other problems.

The world continually provides new wicked problems—our complex business environment is the epitome of "incomplete, contradictory, and changing requirements."[2] Your clients

---

[2] https://en.wikipedia.org/wiki/Wicked_problem.

and mine struggle to change in part because there is no single solution to such problems and, I would argue, no certainty of improvement.

One of the largest reasons your clients don't act on the problems you are used to solving is because they lack certainty. Your One-Up position will allow you to help them make sense of their complex situation and provide a higher-resolution lens, bringing in more light and greater clarity of vision. Combined with the other strategies that enable One-Upness, you will allow your clients to see things in a way that permits them to move forward.

The reason professional selling continually evolves is because we are—and have been—helping clients solve their challenges and problems forever. As our clients' problems grow in complexity and difficulty, our approaches must change in response. The change that we are just beginning to pursue is a momentous leap forward, one that requires solving a new set of problems. These new problems only feel wicked because as a profession we haven't done much work to address them. As you develop and practice One-Up strategies, you'll be better equipped to solve your clients' wicked problems— and you'll become a "sense maker," someone who can make sense of the gnarly web of complexity that your clients are stuck in.

Handling Your Habitat

David Snowden, a Welsh management consultant whose work I first discovered when he co-authored a paper with Gary Klein, created a framework for how best to respond to your environment. The framework is called Cynefin, a Welsh word that means "habitat." Like apparently every management framework, this one divides decision-making into four quadrants.

1. **Simple:** When the cause and effect is known, the right response is to sense, categorize, and respond. Here, best practices dominate.

2. **Complicated:** When things are complicated, you need to analyze the relationship between cause and effect. The right response is to sense, analyze, and respond. Here, good practices dominate decisions.
3. **Complex:** What makes something complex is that the relationship between cause and effect is only clear in hindsight. Here, you probe, sense, and respond.
4. **Chaotic:** Chaos represents the idea that the relationship between cause and effect is at the systems level. In this case, you act first, sense, and then respond.

Nobody ever said that being One-Up would be easy! While you don't need to be an expert on chaos theory or complexity, you need to know that you create value for your clients by helping them probe, sense, and respond effectively. My theory is that most clients recognize that they need to address their problems and challenges, but they continue to struggle because they are uncertain about the context and outcomes. The need for consensus before taking any action or pursuing any kind of change initiative makes this even more difficult. Helping one person secure certainty about moving forward is one thing, but repeating the process with thirteen other people—while keeping everyone heading in the same direction—is a problem of a different magnitude.

As we've seen, being One-Up requires you to lead your client, starting with your insights, to correct the information disparity that prevents them from making the best decision for their business. Now we can add another strategic superpower: sense-making.

Sense-Making and One-Upness

In the past, you needed to be an expert when it came to your company, your products, and maybe your industry. Now, success requires more of you. You need to be One-Up in ways that solve the problems that prevent your client from being able to change. Before we get into sense-making as a practice, you need to know that there are a lot of different frameworks for understanding and even defining sense-making. The term was coined by Karl E. Weick, an organizational theorist, who put it in terms of how people give meaning to their experiences. For our purposes, sense-making means helping your clients understand their world well enough that they can take the actions necessary to change. (Note: The sense-making framework here is based on one from InnerVentures,[3] with additions of my own.)

First, let's look at the main inputs.

- **Information.** There is now more data than ever. While you might believe that more data should provide more insight, conflicting data and perspectives can make it more difficult to know who or what to believe. As the sense maker, you select the data your client needs to understand the nature of their problem and how to make sense of their world.
- **Experience.** Both you and your prospective client have experience. What makes you One-Up is that you have more experience helping solve the kind of problems they have. That experience provides you with a deeper understanding of what's going on, the implications for your prospect, what's working, what's not, and how to evaluate options.

Given these inputs, your sense-making should consider several elements.

---

[3] Stephen Danelutti, "Making Sense of Sensemaking," InnerVentures, May 31, 2016. Available at: https://innerventur.es/2016/05/31/making-sense-of-sensemaking/.

- **Value.** The first step in sense-making is to discern the value of the inputs when it comes to helping your clients understand their world. You want to identify the trends and forces that explain what's going on.
- **Implications.** This is a two-fer. First, you want to identify the implications for your clients. Second, you want to judge the impact on your contacts as it pertains to improving their understanding.
- **Time Value.** Sense-making inputs should help explain why things are the way they are now, as well as pointing to what the future holds for your clients.

Finally, here are the key outputs of your sense-making.

- **Theory.** Your sense-making provides you with a theory about what's going on. Your theory is made up of your knowledge, your experience, and your insights.
- **Narrative.** One of the ways we make sense of our environment is through stories—whether they're news stories, commentaries, or even fairy tales. A compelling narrative is one of the ways you provide your client with a higher-resolution lens.
- **Strategies.** Ideally, sense-making should result in a strategy to move forward, based on a renewed understanding of your client's environment and how best to respond to it now.
- **Actions.** When you can make sense of your client's world for them, you open up the opportunity to provide them with your advice and your recommendations, identifying specific actions they need to take to improve their position.

The Institute for the Future, writing in the University of Phoenix Research Institute's "Future Work Skills 2020" report, listed sense-making as the number-one future work skill. They defined sense-making as the "ability to determine the deeper meaning or significance of what is being expressed." Number 2 on their list was social intelligence, defined as the "ability to connect to others in a deep and direct way, to sense and stimulate reactions and desired interactions." Number 3 was novel and adaptive thinking, defined as "proficiency at thinking and coming up with solutions and responses beyond what is rote, or rules based."

All three should sound familiar: The future is custom-made for One-Up salespeople, but it won't be kind to those who are One-Down.

Start Making Sense

Providing your clients with a higher-resolution lens means helping them with a number of outcomes you have not been trained, coached, or enabled to address. Unfortunately, this means that both you and your prospective clients are One-Down, but only for a few more chapters. After that, you will be One-Up and better prepared to help lift your client out of their One-Down position. You have to be an expert in explaining the intersection where your company and your clients meet. You don't have to be an expert on your client's business, but you do have to be an expert at explaining the trends, forces, and factors that explain your client's world.

Let me demonstrate how you might make sense of your client's world, using B2B sales as an example. At the time of this writing, here's what the world of B2B buying looked like:

- *Harvard Business Review* suggested that 70 percent of all B2B change initiatives fail.[4]

---

[4] Nadya Zhexembayeva, "3 Things You're Getting Wrong About Organizational Change," *Harvard Business Review*, June 9, 2020.

- There is evidence showing that only 5 percent of digital transformations meet their objectives.[5]
- B2B salespeople get approximately 5 percent of a buyer's time. Gartner's research shows that buyers spend 27 percent of their time doing online research and 17 percent with potential partners.[6]

In this context, we're asking and answering two big questions: 1) What are we doing—or allowing our clients to do—that cause them to fail? 2) What should we do—or stop doing—to command more of their time and enable better outcomes? Let's map this onto the component parts of sense-making:

- **Information and Experience.** I chose the information I believed would provide you with the higher-resolution lens I wanted you to look through based on B2B. The reason I cited my sources is because it is important for you to know that I am sharing my informed opinion with you, one that is supported by evidence from third parties. Through this higher-resolution lens, I helped you to see the challenges of buying and selling, giving evidence that we are not providing our clients the help they need to tackle their problems.
- **Implications.** It's unlikely that you were already aware of the trends, forces, and factors making things more difficult for buyers and their organizations and harm their results, mostly because we don't talk about these things enough. There are other trends, forces, and factors in play, but I chose the ones I believed created the greatest impact and time value.

---

[5] Laurent-Pierre Baculard et al., "Orchestrating a Successful Digital Transformation," Bain & Company, November 22, 2017.
[6] Gartner, "The Chief Sales Officer's Leadership Vision for 2021" webinar (n.d.).

- **Theory.** My perspective suggests that the central challenge of professional sales is creating meaningful value for our clients as it pertains to their decisions. This theory is based on my experience and supported by strong evidence.
- **The Narrative.** The narrative is the story about what clients need from salespeople, why some salespeople are unable to meet their needs, and what one might need to change to improve both their clients' results and their own. Deep down, I believe that most salespeople truly want to help their clients improve, but they haven't yet been enabled to do so in a way that is right for today's business environment.

  The questions that follow the facts and data above suggest that there are ways to tame these wicked problems and bring them under control. The approach here not only provides a higher-resolution lens, but also provides the view that your clients can do something about those problems—provided they have the counsel, advice, and recommendations of a person who is One-Up enough to help.
- **Strategies and Actions.** As you already know, the major strategy here is using your One-Up ability and willingness to help your clients close the gaps in their knowledge and experience, starting by helping them to understand their world.

Why Decision Makers and Decision Shapers Seek Trusted Advisors

Aristotle tutored Alexander the Great, providing him the wisdom to allow the peoples he conquered to keep their customs and their cultures. It was essentially a higher-resolution lens through which to view human nature, and he used it to take some of the sting out of removing his enemies' political autonomy.

Harry Hopkins was President Franklin Delano Roosevelt's Secretary of Commerce. Roosevelt relied so heavily on Hopkins's advice that Winston Churchill went directly to Hopkins to help him persuade Roosevelt to enter World War II. Hopkins helped Roosevelt by providing a lens on the political and geopolitical world, shaping his view.

Warren Buffett changed his approach to investing on the advice of Charlie Munger, who counseled him to buy great companies and hold them forever—replacing the advice of Buffett's first advisor, Benjamin Graham. Munger's advice provided Buffett a sharper lens through which to view investment decisions. In the decades since, Munger's advice has been worth hundreds of billions.

As these examples show, successful people surround themselves with advisors who can provide them with a clearer view of their world and their decisions. They want to be able to see around corners, predict the future, and position themselves and their enterprises to succeed.

We return now to one of the central ideas in this book: The sales conversation is your only vehicle for creating value for your clients. If your client doesn't trust your advice, they won't buy from you. To gain that trust, you must give them a lens that provides a clearer view of their world and how best to approach the decisions required to navigate it.

Imagine two salespeople competing for a client's business. The first salesperson focuses on eliciting the client's primary problem, a problem that has harmed their performance for their customers. This salesperson tells their company's story with a skill that rivals Martin Scorsese (I know, I know; no one really rivals Scorsese). The salesperson has a tremendous command of their company's solution, explaining perfectly how and why it is the best fit for the prospective client.

The second salesperson, instead of asking the client about their existing problem, explains to the client the trends and forces causing their problems. In doing so, he provides a higher-resolution lens through which the buyer sees their world and the decisions they need to make to improve their results. The problem looks different though this new lens, an outcome that the first salesperson didn't provide. Instead of positioning their solution, the second salesperson provides advice and recommendations about solving problems in the first place.

The first salesperson's advice and recommendations are limited to "buy my solution from me and my company and we'll solve your problem." The second person's advice and recommendations are to "look through this lens to gain a clearer picture of your problem, then consider this response to improve your results." You want to be the second salesperson, not the first. You want to be the one who helps your client see something that was not visible to them until you brought in a sharper lens and opened their aperture to let in greater light and more detail, without losing sight of the big picture.

You don't want to sell in a way that allows you to merely win a deal, a project, or an order. Instead, set your sights on winning the client. Once you've established yourself as a One-Up advisor, by improving your client's view of the world and their outcomes, you no longer have to compete for future deals. To earn an absolute, unassailable right to the next deal, you must provide the lens that shapes your client's view—capturing not just income but mindshare. In fact, truly One-Up sales will retire the category for the decision-makers, decision-shapers, and the stakeholders whom you help, as they'll happily let you guide them for years to come.

Your company, your product, your services, your solution, the list of your clients, a map of your locations, your other clients' references and testimonials, and the clever way you elicit your prospective client's problem—none of this is advice, and none of it will help you become your client's trusted advisor. Instead, you must offer a better view of their reality and the decisions before them, positioning yourself as a sense maker and a potential trusted advisor.

6

The Advantage of Your Vantage Point

A single vantage point is an absurdly narrow vantage point from which to view the world.

—Aleister Crowley

As I WARNED you at the start of this book, the main threats to being One-Up are hubris and arrogance. Consider, for example, the tone in this paragraph:

> Were I to decide which one of us should determine what steps to take to improve your results, I would humbly insist that I should lead the process, given that I am One-Up and you are One-Down. You might believe that you should be able to have a say in this process, since you desire better results, a position I fully appreciate and support. Any conflict around the process would result from your attempt to circumvent some important conversation or commitment, in which case, I should decide for you, and you should defer to my judgment.

Now, I hope you never use this specific language when talking to your clients. Despite its thin veneer of humility, bordering on servile obsequiousness, every word in the paragraph is about making your audience feel One-Down, so they never forget your superior abilities and certainly never see you as a partner. That's why one rule for being One-Up is never make the other person feel One-Down. But as cringy as the paragraph is, you must believe every word of it and allow every idea to drive your actions.

You must lead your client through the conversations they need to reach the outcomes they want, and you can't stop leading just because there's conflict or even a challenge to your authority. But the best leaders are often the best diplomats. In this situation, for instance, you could execute the same move by asking a simple question: "Can I share with you what my concern is and help you ensure you can move forward, without having to worry about some of the challenges that will prevent you from generating the better results you need?" No arrogance, no hubris, no conflict. Instead, counsel, advice, and suggestions.

You cannot guide your clients without leading them, but you cannot truly lead them if every conversation is about your own superiority. As we explore how to utilize your One-Up vantage point to facilitate a needs-based buyer's journey, please don't forget that your language and your attitude matter just as much as your insights.

Your Sales Problem Is a Buying Problem

You've probably heard that to succeed in sales, you need only "sell good products and solve your client's problems." While those things help, that general strategy—the legacy solution approach—actually prevents salespeople and sales organizations from producing better results because it underserves their clients. The "sell the problem, solve the problem" approach limits your ability to occupy the One-Up position because it doesn't allow you to see what actually stops you from winning deals: your client's buying problem.

To be One-Up, you must distinguish between two kinds of problems. On one hand, there are the presenting problems your contacts are experiencing that you are well-prepared to solve—things like labor shortages, inefficient logistics, poor communication, or low employee morale. But on the other hand, there are deep-seated, strategic challenges that prevent them from successfully changing and improving their outcomes. One-Down salespeople often pick up on the first kind of problem but aren't even aware of the second kind. But if you can't help your clients improve their problem-solving in the first place, it won't matter how many solutions you have for their presenting problems.

No matter how you were taught and trained to sell, chances are that your sales processes and sales methodologies are concerned with your own success, not with meeting your client's needs.

In fact, all the hype about "the sales process" was that it would provide a repeatable, paint-by-numbers way to win deals, helping every salesperson reach their goals. Thus, sales enablement became about improving the salesperson's ability to follow directions and (somehow) improve their effectiveness. Neither process helps your contacts and stakeholders buy in a way that ensured they succeeded. In fact, for decades, few sales organizations paid serious attention to the challenges their client companies have with buying.

Without ever having seen the slide deck that outlines your sales process, I can tell you what it includes: "target," "qualify," "discovery," "presentation," "negotiation," and "won/lost." If you use Salesforce.com, you have eleven stages that include "market-qualified lead," "sales-qualified lead," and a number of stages that are even more unnecessary, except to give marketing their props. Tell me if these steps sound all too familiar: "awareness of a problem," "exploration," "evaluation," "purchase," and if your marketing team has optimistic cheerleaders or is located somewhere close to Silicon Valley, the last stage is "evangelist."

Those models aren't all bad; they at least give you a way to know where you are in space and provide some direction about where to go. I have always been dubious about linear sales processes, believing that a dynamic conversation doesn't lend itself to simplified models. While there is nothing inherently wrong with outlining the sales process and the buyer's journey, the view of sales enablement is not the view of buyer enablement and has proven inadequate to helping companies change and improve their results. I am even more convinced now that One-Up agility beats a slide deck any day.

The Worst Advice for Salespeople

A friend wrote a LinkedIn post that included the statement "Salespeople need to sell the way buyers want to buy." I was admittedly triggered and fired off a comment, condemning his idea as incredibly dangerous and largely responsible for poor B2B results. What clients say they want on surveys by insight-based groups doesn't match their behaviors, especially with big companies. Your clients don't know that they are skipping conversations and making it less likely they will succeed. Following that advice cements the salesperson in a One-Down position: compliant, reactive, servile, and ready to take orders like a fast-food cashier. If all you do is take (or follow!) your client's orders, you can't create value for them.

It's time to raise the bar on how you engage with your clients. Think of it this way. You spend every working day guiding companies to the better results they need. Your client changes only occasionally, giving them very little expertise about how best to decide, what factors they need to consider, what steps are necessary, and what choice will serve them the best. Because you have more experience, you should lead a facilitated, needs-based, buyer's journey.

The word "facilitated" means you will lead your contacts and the other stakeholders who are part of the conversation. "Needs-based" means that you will recognize what your prospect needs to do to successfully decide and improve their results. Like my Sherpa at Basecamp One, you have guided many people to the summit, helping them arrive there safely. Your client rarely even visits the mountain, so allowing them to lead the climb is almost certain to end badly. Your contacts are bright people with a lot of experience, but you are One-Up because you have much greater experience making the decision you will ask them to make, the one that will move their business forward.

Before we describe the facilitated, needs-based buyer's journey in more detail, let's look at why buyers can't—or don't—buy.

Why Buyers Can't Buy

An enormous number of challenges prevent buyers from changing, even when the change is necessary. Whatever problem your product or service solves, you must first deal with the complications that prevent your decision-makers and shapers from acting. Being One-Up, you are perfectly positioned to identify and resolve these complications, allowing your prospect to move forward in the sales conversation and, eventually, improve their position. Here's what to look for.

- **Uncertainty.** By default, your clients will struggle to choose change when they're experiencing uncertainty. The fact that your "solution" might solve the presenting problem does nothing to solve the problem of uncertainty. In later chapters you'll learn how to create the certainty of negative consequences, then eventually create the certainty of better results and transformation.
- **A Limited Understanding.** Many of your clients understand little about their problem and even less about how they should address it. They may feel ill-equipped to propose or decide on a change. When they don't know enough about the situation, the easiest decision is to do nothing and wait for better information. If that's the case, you educate your client, giving them at least a working understanding of their problem. I know something you don't know; may I share it?
- **Misalignment.** One challenge of strategic decision-making is misalignment. When a group of leaders can't agree on how to move forward—or worse, when their priorities conflict—they often end in a stalemate, one that leaves problems and challenges unaddressed far longer than they should have. There is no sales process or buyer's journey that recognizes or addresses these or similar conflicts. Your vantage point allows you to lead your client in resolving them.
- **Lack of Consensus.** Even when a group will pursue change, they can struggle to acquire consensus, a second path to a stalemate that allows both their results and their team members to suffer. Let me be as direct as I can: When you are

working toward being One-Up, it is your responsibility to lead your client in building the consensus they need.

- **Limited Emotional Energy.** We underestimate how much emotional energy our clients must invest in change. Much of that energy is spent on conflict-heavy conversations that we are neither part of nor privy to, even though our initiative prompted the conflict. You need to provide a different level of support that bolsters them psychologically when they run headlong into discord. Your absence is felt, but so is your presence.

- **Limited Time.** It's essential to recognize that your client's main responsibility is running their business. They are almost sure to be time-starved and already saddled with more work and more demands for communication than they can handle in the course of a day, a week, or a year. Too little time dooms many an initiative, so you must command more time by effectively addressing your contact's needs, always helping them take one step forward.

- **Position and Blame.** It is not uncommon for people to avoid change, especially in political environments. Any failure might cause a contact to lose status or have others exploit their weakness. A tough start on a new initiative is enough to cause anyone to think twice before committing to future change. After all, you are up against a history of salespeople who failed to provide a buyer's journey that ended in success.

The list of complications above isn't anywhere close to complete, but it should put you on the trail of whatever your buyers do that keeps them from successfully changing. You can't solve what you can't see. My thesis is that 70 percent of change initiatives fail because the company treated what is a complex buying decision as something merely transactional. Trying to sell like buyers want to buy leaves you in the One-Down position, taking orders—and failing your client by allowing them to fail.

A Facilitated, Needs-Based Buyer's Journey

Let us turn the spotlight on the buyer's journey, since that is the context in which your vantage point is most valuable. Your sales conversation is your best vehicle for enabling this journey, but you must actively facilitate it by identifying what your client needs to move forward. Let's look at a practical, tactical, non-marketing-department-designed buyer's journey.

The first stage of the buyer's journey is not awareness. You must reject the One-Down belief that your client has to suffer negative consequences before you can offer help. Instead, demonstrate your proactive ability to compel change before your client experiences the harm that might otherwise cause them to change. Your approach will differ depending on where you find your client.

- **Not Compelled.** The largest percentage of companies you call on will be those who are not yet compelled to change, even though they probably should be. Since none of us knows what we don't know, your contacts need you to help them recognize the storm clouds gathering, while they still have time to act. Even when a company and their decision-makers are obstinate, continue to call on them and capture mindshare by helping them see the negative future that awaits them. Later, you will be the prescient person who predicted their future.
- **Compelled and Confused.** When you show up late for your clients and prospects, you may find they are already experiencing the residual poor results of their inactivity, leaving them unable to keep pace with the demands of their environment. They either didn't change soon enough or something in their world changed so fast they didn't have time to respond effectively. Here, you need to facilitate a conversation that provides your buyers with a deeper understanding of the nature

of their challenge and offer them a chance to explore change. The value system that underpins this approach is that you are obligated to proactively help your client change.

- **Compelled and Experienced.** That these stakeholders are both compelled and experienced is an indication that something has changed. When your contacts are already compelled, you don't have to work to compel them to change, although you do want to help them understand what's changed outside their windows, and the nature of their challenge.

No matter what your clients are experiencing, there are certain things that will benefit them. When you're One-Up, you will be able to give you buyers the things they need, including the following:

- **Exploring Change.** Your client generally benefits from help exploring what choices they might make to improve their results: the factors they need to consider, what they will need to do to improve their results, and how best to achieve their objectives. Facilitating this conversation means being truly consultative, suggesting what they need to consider and why it will be important to their future success. This a powerful use of your vantage point and your experience.

- **Self-Discovery.** While it is important to understand what your contacts need during discovery, they must also discover something about their business and how best to build better results. Your business acumen, experience, and insights will help your clients work toward a solution. They will also need your help facilitating the design of the initiative you undertake together, ensuring they can execute it and produce the results they need.

- **Executing an Effective Buyer's Journey.** Many contacts have gaps in their knowledge when it comes to the conversations and commitments they need to have to make a good decision. As you discovered earlier, some of the most important insights you possess are "buying insights," the conversations that are necessary for your client to effectively decide.

- **Investing Wisely.** Until you help your buyers recognize the investment necessary to improve their results, they will only see your price. Your buyers should be able to understand both why they need to invest and what consequences they face for underinvesting in their solution—preventing the concessions that come with an investment inadequate for the results they require.

- **Moving Forward.** Your buyers need to see a solution that they agree will work for them. But even more important, they need the certainty they will succeed—and that you are prepared to ensure that they do not fail. Like Scrooge's ghosts, you aid them when you remind them of their current state, show their future state, help them understand what challenges they should expect, and explain how you will help them overcome any obstacles. The One-Up position requires that you create certainty of outcome for your clients.

Maps of the Sales Conversation

Maps are valuable because they let you recognize where you are and plot a path to where you need to go. The traditional sales process functions the same way. It doesn't provide your prospective clients with a tremendous amount of value, especially if you perceive a sale as a straight line, but it does remind you of some things you need to do to enable your clients to succeed.

In my book *The Lost Art of Closing: Winning the Ten Commitments That Drive Sales*, you will find a very different map of the sales conversation. The chapters follow a pattern you might recognize: not a linear set of instructions, but ten conversations your prospective client needs to make a good decision and execute an initiative that provides them with better outcomes. I've included a shortened version of the map below. Hopefully, it will help you recognize when your prospective clients are trying to skip critical conversations, avoid the decisions they need to make, and post-pone the actions they need to take.

- **Time.** The first commitment a client needs to make is the commitment of time. During your first meeting, you provide your prospective client with insights that help them better understand their changing world and the potential implica-tions. In a later chapter you will find another tactic designed to help you compel your clients to change before their results or their business is harmed. You can use these tactics to start your client on their buyer's journey, to prevent them from waiting until they are already challenged by problems and issues that harm them.

- **Explore.** Once your prospective client recognizes their chal-lenges, they often want to explore the better results avail-able to them, and what gaining those results might require of them. The fact that you are One-Up allows you to teach them how to explore the changes they may need to make. You facilitate this conversation and help them recognize their future potential.

- **Change.** One reason deals stall is because clients often avoid the commitment to change, the decision to move forward in their journey. This conversation may take time to develop, and it may mean you have to get a little further down the path before your client can commit to change. This is one challenge of a nonlinear conversation and deciding in a com-plex environment, and you help by recognizing which con-versations may be helpful.

- **Collaborate.** Helping a client change always requires a col-laborative conversation about what they might need to change, what is the right approach, and whether it will work for their company and their teams. One of the ways you can make it easy for your client and their team to buy from you is by including them in the design of the project or initiative that will improve their results.

■ **Build consensus.** The larger, more complex, and more strategic the decision, the more your conversation will include the need to build consensus from the client's teams and stakeholders. The ability to lead this process requires that you are fully One-Up and leading; many of your clients will see this conversation as a threat to their authority, but the real danger is that they leave people out and cause them to withhold their support or actively work against their efforts.

To remind you about nonlinearity, I want to remind you that at any time, starting with your first conversation, you may find your main contact asking their peers to join the conversation. More broadly, you don't always get to control when your clients pursue some of the outcomes they believe they need. They may also hit you with a barrage of concerns about the path you are leading them down or about the change they need to make. Overall, you may have to facilitate the consensus conversation when it occurs, not when you believe it makes the most sense.

■ **Invest.** At some point, you have to talk to your client about the investment you're asking them to make in the better results they need. Like consensus, you may need to discuss investment relatively earlier or later in the sales conversation. I have always found that it is easier to share a higher price earlier in the conversation than surprising your client with it at the end. I prefer to use the entire sales conversation to prove the greater value of the outcomes my company can create when compared to a competitor (see Chapter 10 on triangulation).

■ **Review.** At some point, you have to present a proposal that can garner the support necessary for you to win your prospective client's business. This is a relatively low-level commitment for your prospective clients, as they are not signing a contract. It's better to get a yes to the question "Will this work?" than to discover it won't when your client calls to tell you they "went another direction," one that is 180 degrees from the path you'd suggested.

- **Resolve Concerns.** Much of the time, after hearing your presentation, your contacts will tell you they will let you know after they meet with their team. Now more than ever, the number of people and the perceived risks that come with a complex business environment generate deal-killing concerns. Without a conversation to identify and resolve those concerns, you risk your client doing nothing. Unresolved concerns kill deals.

- **Decide.** Asking the client to buy from you is among the easiest of these commitments if you have created value through the conversation. If you haven't, the Gods of Sales will mock your efforts and mark your deal Closed-Lost.

Now you have a One-Up map that presumes you are not going straight from point A to point B with no real challenges. Instead, it provides you with a way to recognize what conversations your client has completed and which ones are still necessary. Your clients may need additional conversations, and they'll probably happen in a different order. Recognizing those variations is part of what makes you One-Up, making your vantage point your client's advantage.

Being One-Up and possessing a useful set of maps allows you to recognize the conversations your clients need to complete their journey, always with your help, and always following your lead. When you recognize that a conversation was skipped or has not been successfully concluded, you must ensure it is completed. You will find that your contacts don't always know who they need to include in these conversations, and they often wait too long to begin the process of important outcomes like building organizational consensus. It is often necessary to explain why your client needs to have the conversations necessary to make the best decision for their business, and how they are critical to successfully conducting the change they need to make.

Obstacles and Pitfalls

The first obstacle you will encounter when trying to share your vantage point will come from clients who believe in—and are committed to—their legacy buying process, even when it harms their decision and their results. Imagine a client who releases an RFP and then meets with three companies, giving each one ninety minutes to make their case in a bake-off. Any process that treats a strategic decision as if it were transactional neutralizes your One-Upness by ensuring you are One-Down.

Because you are One-Up (or will be after practicing these strategies), you have the knowledge and skills to disrupt this arm's-length process in a meaningful and diplomatic way. You are not doing so out of some sort of malice—though I would understand your emotional response to a value-eliminating process—but to prevent your prospective client from making a mistake that would be easily avoided.

The One-Up strategy for disrupting the RFP process is to read the RFP from the end, searching for something you can use to complain about the way the questions and prompts are written. (This should not be difficult, since most RFPs are usually based on a template not updated since the Clinton administration.) Once you discover something to gripe about, call the person who sent you the RFP, and ask them a question they cannot answer. Here's a good one: "I am not sure how to respond to some of your questions. A number of them are written in a way that doesn't allow us to answer them. How do you want us to describe the way we do these things now to lower costs and provide a better result?" The game you are playing here is called "I know something you don't know." Just like that, your contact is now in the One-Down position, especially if they feel like they are missing something they might have been expected to know.

If you are really One-Up you should call the person who is going to care most about the results the RFP is designed to deliver, instead of calling the purchasing department. When you call an executive, you tell them their RFP has problems and ask them to intervene with the purchasing function, to allow you to provide a newer, better approach that they will want to consider. At worst, you will get a second look. One reason executives prefer to work with people who are One-Up is that it allows them to outsource the expertise they lack. When you make sure your clients know what they need to know, you prevent them from having to worry about the area you have covered for them.

Another challenge comes from the intermediaries who stand between you and the people you intend to serve. Third parties, brokers, and professional buyers are paid to treat every purchase as if they were buying a bushel of apples. No matter how complex the purchase, no matter how important the results, it's just another transaction to them. There is only one way to get in front of third parties and that is a strategy called Year Zero. The Year Zero strategy starts the day your target client signs a three-year contract with your competitor. That very day, you start a campaign to create relationships with the people who made that decision. Your One-Down competitors will sit passively, waiting for the three years to end so they can fill out another RFP. Getting this right means creating more—and deeper—relationships than the third party, the broker, or their purchasing agent. You will find you have little trouble being One-Up over any third party, especially one that lacks your expertise.

Never let it be said that I believe that anything I write about is easy to execute. But all these strategies are necessary and especially important to being One-Up—and you can quote me on that.

The key is explaining to your contacts what they need to do and the value it will bring them. Being One-Up means using your vantage point to explain the value of what you are asking your client to do, the potential negative consequences for avoiding that action, and the positive outcomes that come from following your instruction.

One sales organization I know found that helping their clients required sixteen different steps. They built a slide deck to show their clients all the things they would need to do together to transform the client's business and their results. They shared their map with their clients, who responded by asking for a copy of the roadmap they would need to follow together. For the first time, their clients recognized that the better results they needed would not be obtained by finding a supplier with a lower price. The adoption of the sales organization's map is proof positive of One-Upness.

Agility and Your (Ad)vantage Point

The complex environment that seems to provide a constant, disruptive, and accelerating change makes it more difficult for people to decide to change, primarily due to a lack of certainty and a reasonable fear of getting a decision wrong. Because this is true, the new competency is one we can call agility. Physically, agility is the ability to move quickly and easily, pivoting when necessary and changing direction on a dime. But it also means being able to think and understand quickly.

The sales process's nonlinear character means you need to recognize where you are, where your client is, and how to serve them. Your vantage point—your understanding of what your client needs from you—provides you and your client an advantage. It unlocks both of you from a static, linear process, opening up the possibility to work together to ensure you reach the summit.

7

Building Your One-Upness

God fights on the side with the best artillery.

—*Napoleon Bonaparte*

NAPOLEON KNEW A thing or two about being One-Up: His battle record was fifty wins and seven losses. Your insights comprise a large part of your "artillery," along with your ability to transfer them to the decision-makers and decision-shapers you serve. In a book titled *Seeing What Others Don't: The Remarkable Ways We Gain Insights*, Dr. Gary Klein provides the best and most complete account of how we acquire insights. Here is how he describes what he calls discontinuous discoveries:

> Insights shift us toward a new story, a new set of beliefs that are more accurate, more comprehensive, and more useful. Our insights transform us in several ways. They change how we understand, act, see, feel, and desire. They change how we understand. They transform our thinking; our new story gives us a different viewpoint. They change how we act. . . . Insights transform how we see; we look for different things in keeping with our new story.[1]

How helpful would it be if you could provide your contacts a new story, one that delivers a new set of beliefs that allow better decisions? What if you could change how your contacts understand their world and provide them with a different viewpoint? In large part, achieving those goals is a matter of securing insights that allow you to occupy the One-Up position.

Klein provides a model of insights that follows one of three paths. The first path is triggered by a contradiction or an inconsistency. To acquire an insight this way, you use a weak anchor

---

[1] Gary Klein, *Seeing What Others Don't: The Remarkable Ways We Gain Insights* (New York: PublicAffairs, 2015), 23–24.

(core belief) to rebuild the story. When you can rebuild your client's story, you change how they understand some part of their world. The second path starts with a correction, a coincidence, or a curiosity, each allowing you to spot an "implication." The activity that gives rise to the insight is adding a new anchor or core belief. This sometimes gives rise to an aha moment. Klein links the final path with "creative desperation," a moment that allows you to "escape an impasse." To create a breakthrough here, you have to escape some problem you are struggling to resolve effectively.

When I was forced into the role of account executive, I was taught and trained in the legacy approaches to sales. I started presentations for my prospective clients by reading the eighty-four-page binder I wrote about earlier. If I had to rank the worst villains in human history, the list would include Hitler, Stalin, Mao, Pol Pot, the inventor of email, and whoever decided we should start client conversations with "why us." That choice—at least in B2B sales—has created much suffering and misery for thousands of innocent professionals who agreed to meet with well-meaning people, only to be left wondering "why me?"

After a brain surgery, I found myself back in Columbus, Ohio, unable to drive for two years, preventing me from resuming my freeway-focused life in Los Angeles. This period of my professional life was peak *solution selling*, which meant adding "why our solution" to "why us." The result was a one-sided conversation that, when done well, cured the worst case of insomnia, often bypassing sleep and going right to a catatonic state immune to the most potent of smelling salts.

At some point, I noticed that these approaches had lost their effectiveness. Their power was fading fast. My first real clue that something changed came at the beginning of a conversation with an enormous prospect in Cincinnati, Ohio. As I sat down in his office, I pulled out my laptop to share my beautiful, fully animated slide deck when my contact said, "I don't want to see your slides. Put your laptop away or this meeting is over.

I just want to ask you some questions." I suddenly found myself in the One-Down position. Later, a friend told me he had a similar experience, with his contact threatening to "throw your ass out of here if you so much as open your laptop."

I knew my approach had to change, so I looked for insights beyond "you should probably buy our solution." My primary insight about the industry I worked in came from Klein's third path: creative desperation. I was trying to persuade a client to spend more money to improve their results. They were paying their employees too little, and they were struggling to run their business. I recognized that my contacts' assumptions were no longer true, and, out of desperation, I decided to prosecute their beliefs, treating my meeting as a sort of trial. I had been collecting "evidence" that they needed to change, and I organized it for presentation.

My contact's two primary false assumptions were: 1) labor is abundant, and 2) labor is cheap. Neither of these assumptions were accurate and hadn't been for a long time. In the course of about 100 slides, I presented data, newspaper articles, government reports and charts, and comparisons of my client's wages versus other local companies' starting wages, and how often (and how much) their competitors increased employee pay. As boring as this might sound to you, they were riveted. At the end of the meeting, for the first time ever, my main contact asked me for my slide deck. He later used it to brief his executive team, calling me afterward to inform me they were raising their pay rates. The increase meant spending two million dollars more annually.

I was One-Up as it pertained to my client's need for higher wages. The knowledge I shared was not some well-guarded secret. Anyone who wanted to acquire that same information would have had little trouble doing so. My perspective, however, was not available to my clients because they had not worked in my industry and lacked the thousands of hours of experience I had accumulated. You will find that, while your clients are One-Up experts in their industry, they don't spend a lot of time research-ing other companies or industries.

I had provided my contacts with a new story, new beliefs, and new actions—actions that improved their results. I changed my approach from "why us" and "why our solution" to "why change." And don't worry; the One-Up approach will equip you to answer "why us" without ever having to say so out loud. If you have to convince your client directly that they should buy from your company, it's a safe bet that you didn't create enough value to earn their business.

After that experience, I never carried the slide deck that included our company's story, the picture of our corporate office, our locations, the logos of the large, well-recognized cli-ents, or our many impressive awards. Instead, I started every conversation with the deck I had assembled to help that pro-spective client understand their world, enabling them to make better decisions and improve their overall results. This was my "artillery," one with power much greater than anything my competitors were using, something I knew for certain when a couple of clients handed me all of my many competitors' collat-eral and their proposals. Naturally, it was all "why us," lacking any insight.

This approach worked for two reasons. First, I was providing my client with a conversation that allowed me to transfer my insights to my contacts, providing them a perspective that led them to better and more informed decisions. Second, because my conversation created a level of value far greater than my legacy approach competitors, I differentiated and distinguished myself from the rest of the field. To be One-Up, you first have to do the work to build your One-Upness. The longer you work in an industry, the easier you will find this work. But first, we will need to outline several approaches with provocative names to ensure you are One-Up.

Obliterating Assumptions

As far as anyone can tell, reality doesn't seem to care about your contact's beliefs, their opinions, their plans, or the assumptions on the spreadsheet that explains their profit model. The universe doesn't seem to be concerned by their opinions or how they think things should work. Yet they cling to their beliefs, even when they are no longer accurate or beneficial. When you notice that your prospect is struggling to produce some necessary result, it invariably means they need to change something they are doing. What prevents smart people from changing is what Klein describes as "anchors," stories they tell themselves. These stories often operate on a set of misconceptions, or what Klein describes as "core beliefs." One of the difficult truths for humans is that we must often choose between our core beliefs and the results we want.

The reason you struggle to help your clients change is not because they aren't smart. It's because you didn't do the work of addressing and replacing their assumptions. The true value of your insights is that they allow you to deal with your client's false assumptions, the ones that come from their limited knowledge and experience. Because you sell the better outcomes your clients need every day, you have the necessary experience to provide a more accurate set of beliefs and stories.

Identifying Implications

This type of insight is not quite as easy to understand as the false assumptions and the stories that anchor them. These insights occur when you recognize a new anchor. The anchor I presented my client with the low wages was a story about how tight the labor market was and how their starting pay rate had fallen behind what was competitive in their market. The implication was that without changing their pay rate, they could not keep their lines running, meaning they would fail their clients, and in one case, have to pay penalties. This was the insight I needed to transfer.

You might notice that decision-makers and decision-shapers reject your advice and recommendations when they clash with their assumptions. Being One-Up means guiding clients to recognize and understand the implications of their assumptions and their decisions. It is easier to accomplish this with facts and data, explaining their reality without directly pointing at the implications. Instead of trying to force the insight on them, you should ideally allow them to come to their own conclusions, recognizing the implications of your briefing. But if you do need to help them recognize the implications, these chapters will provide guidance and language to do so. As the person who is One-Up and responsible for helping those who are currently One-Down, you need to recognize the implications of your client's poor or obsolete assumptions. You can work backward from the negative consequences your clients experience that cause them to change, recognizing and categorizing the implications of your client's false assumptions and poor decisions.

Erasing Mistakes in Advance

Being One-Up requires that you prevent your clients from making mistakes they could avoid by following your guidance. Your advantage is that you have witnessed different companies make different decisions, observing both their mistakes and their successes. This situational knowledge is unavailable to your One-Down clients and prospects because their experience is limited to a single data point, their company. You may not recognize your One-Upness with client mistakes, especially if you believe your client is One-Up in your relationship. But if you'll consent to being One-Down for few minutes, I will explain why you are One-Up when it comes to the decisions your clients make.

When you pursue a prospective client, their willingness to meet is evidence they know they need better results. There are several reasons your prospective client may be struggling to produce the results they need, but when you seek the ground truth (the root cause), you will find a mistake. Here are two common mistakes you will recognize.

- **Mistaken Investments.** Let's start with the client who assumes that the greatest value results from paying the lowest price. By accepting the lowest price, this variety of client also committed to a set of concessions that the salesperson never disclosed to them. It is only later that the client discovers they made a mistake by underinvesting in the results they needed. In a later chapter, you'll learn how to correct this mistake.
- **Avoiding Change.** Another common mistake is the strong belief that changing one's supplier and solution is all that is necessary to produce better results. In some industries, especially the one where I spent the most time selling, this idea caused companies to change suppliers every quarter, always believing the supplier was the root cause of their poor results. Once I found my way to One-Up, I removed the idea that I was failing my client and presented them with a better set of assumptions, allowing them to see where they were to blame for their poor results. Had I not done so, they would have replaced my company with a competitor, a decision that would not have improved their results.

Listing the mistakes your clients make can help you reverse-engineer their assumptions that led to the negative consequences they were experiencing when you found them. One practice that will accelerate your One-Upness is organizing your experience by writing down your clients' assumptions, the outcomes that stemmed from those assumptions, and the poorly informed decisions that followed.

Constructing the Context for Decisions

To help your contacts improve and change in some meaningful way, you must construct a view of your client's world by providing the context that surrounds their challenges and their decisions. What you share needs to unlock new beliefs, new potential, new decisions, and better results. There is little chance you have been taught or trained to provide your prospective clients with the context necessary to making good decisions. This isn't something that companies enable in their sales force, which is why doing the work to be One-Up gives you an incredible advantage.

One factor that makes you One-Up is that you have a more complete view of your client's reality than they do. The reason companies hire consulting firms is so they can gain counsel from someone with knowledge and experience they lack. A good consultant will see things that their clients can't yet see. The fact that you have greater knowledge and experience allows you to construct the context and show your contacts their business and results through a higher-resolution lens.

The Sources of Power

Here we return to Gary Klein's work, this time looking at his research and experience in *Sources of Power: How People Make Decisions*. The book is about how people decide under pressure, but it offers us an understanding of what is necessary to an insight-based, modern sales approach. What Klein discovered was something called "recognition-primed decisions."[2] Recognizing sources of power in sales will help you locate and develop value-creating insights. We will also consider how each source boosts your One-Upness, because power only accrues to those with experience.

---

[2] Gary Klein, *Sources of Power: How People Make Decisions*, 20th Anniversary Edition (MIT Press: Cambridge, MA: MIT Press, 1999), 15.

Unnoticed Patterns

Your brain recognizes patterns, including patterns that may not be accessible to your conscious mind. Your brain's primary function is to keep you alive, and a large part of pattern recognition occurs in your subconscious mind, allowing you to act on something without making a conscious choice. When you have sold for some time, you recognize patterns you would have missed when you lacked the experience necessary to see them. This is one reason you find yourself far in front of your client when it comes to what they need to do to improve their results. You quickly see a pattern that provides you with the information you need to know how best to help your client improve their results. The One-Up strategy means helping your client through a process of discovering what you already know, slowing down when you realize you are too far out in front of your contacts and helping them catch up. If you want your clients to do what you recommend, you first have to help them see what you see.

What are the patterns you see clearly that your clients don't recognize?

Anomalies or Unexpected Events

In Klein's work, you find a lot of stories about firefighters. Klein was trying to understand how people make decisions under pressure. One story has a fire chief removing his team from a house fire minutes before the floor they were standing on collapsed. When they arrived on the scene, the firefighters expected to find a fire in the kitchen; they walked around looking for flames, but saw nothing. The fire chief's experience of this fire violated his expectations. The living room was too hot and there was no sound. Had the fire been in the kitchen, the living room would not have been so hot, and they would have heard the flames. This fire was silent, and the chief pulled his team out just in time.

The ability to detect anomalies is a source of power. Recognizing when something deviates from the norm draws your attention, clashing with your experience and the general pattern you expect. A friend asked me to help him understand why his team was losing deals after being invited to present to their prospective clients. They were losing every contest, even after the clients said nice things about them. At worst, you would expect, say, a 12 percent win rate from an RFP process. But it wasn't what happened in the presentation that lost this sales team every deal. It was what *didn't* happen. The salespeople had never called on the client before being invited to present, and none of the contacts sitting across the table had ever met them before they walked into the room. One question revealed what "didn't happen." You are One-Up when you can recognize anomalies, things that happened, or things that didn't happen. A large part of your insights comes from recognizing when something violates your expectations or your experience.

What anomalies do you notice that provide you with value-creating insight?

The Big Picture

The ability to grasp the big picture means you understand what's most important and how it will affect other things. In part, you can think of this as recognizing "second-order effects," or the future consequences for making—or not making—a certain decision. This is a large component of constructing the context for your One-Down decision-makers. Your power is helping the client see the big picture, something that is necessary when your client depends only on their own experience, which provides a much smaller picture.

I once had a prospective client who was underinvesting in the result they needed. They discounted many factors, like the availability of labor and the increasing pay rates in their area. From my outside perspective, I was able to see aspects of the environment that they were missing, and I could share that information with them. The vast majority of your clients will appreciate your providing them with the big picture and preventing mistakes.

What are the elements of the big picture that your clients don't yet see, and how can you provide them with the context necessary to the decisions they need to make?

The Way Things Work

When you have worked in an industry or a profession for some time, you know "how things work." This recognition includes information about why one decision provides better results and another decision that, while seeming to make sense, produces poor results. Knowing how things work lets you create tremendous value for your clients as they decide. While your client is almost certain to have the same pattern recognition you have in their industry, you have a greater recognition of how things work in your industry— and more important, in the areas where your two businesses come together to produce results. Generally, people like to understand how things work, so being One-Up is helpful for your clients.

What can you teach your clients about how things work?

Events that Already Happened or Will Happen

Much of the time, your clients are head down doing their work. They don't recognize that certain events have already occurred that will cause them problems in the future. Recognizing the events that have already happened and informing your clients about what they should do in response is valuable to your contacts, especially when you are proactive about helping them change. How we used to think about our power in sales was to lean on our ability to solve a client's problem. In this case, you'd wait for your client to be "dissatisfied," the goal of solution selling. One source of your One-Up power is recognizing when (and how) things have changed and helping your clients before they are harmed.

This is your ability to see around corners, accurately predicting your prospective client's future. Your prescience allows you to help your clients and your prospective clients avoid problems and take advantage of any opportunities made possible by some event or some change in the environment. I make very few predictions and only in areas where I have knowledge and a great deal of experience. Starting a prediction journal can help you recognize when your assumptions are false, improving your ability to predict the future with greater accuracy.

Where to Find Insights

While your clients are busy running their businesses, you should be busy building your One-Upness, and by that I mean the knowledge that will drive your insights. These insights come from different sources.

Outside Your Four Walls

I am not a professional researcher, and I am not suggesting that you should don a lab coat or spend a lot of time camped out in the stacks at your local university's research library. I would, however, insist that you read widely, pay attention to news stories that would affect your clients, and develop a set of deep insights that allow you to see something your client can't yet see, making your One-Up perspective valuable to them.

Forces That Impact Your Client's Results

There are always external forces that will affect your clients, sometimes positive, other times negative. You can use something simple like a PESTLE analysis, where you look at political, economic, scientific, technological, legal, and environmental forces. I recommend you start your day listening to *Squawk Box*, with

Becky Quick, Joe Kernen, and Andrew Ross Sorkin. First, you will avoid the icky partisan lens through which much of the news is filtered, allowing you to escape the divisive nature of media. Second, nearly every show will give you an insight useful for maintaining your information disparity and providing you with a way to create value for your contacts.

Trend Lines That Provide Challenges and Opportunities

Besides the forces that impact your client's results, you also want to pay attention to trend lines. The *Wall Street Journal*, for example, recently published an article that stated there are 700,000 open sales jobs and younger generations don't want them.[3] Another trend I follow is the percentage of salespeople who meet quota, a trend line pointing sharply down, and one I would argue can be cured only by being One-Up.

Predictors and Predictions

There are people who study industries thoroughly, then publish their findings and their predictions. They write blog posts with titles like "The Ten Trends That Will Impact the Healthcare Industry in 2022." I call these folks synthesizers; the best ones read deeply, publishing their findings with links to their sources. The pro tip here is to find conflicting perspectives. That dramatically improves your One-Up perspective because it allows you to understand a trend or issue from a variety of perspectives. That way, you can help your client fully consider the implications of their decision, including aspects that they might overlook.

---

[3] Patrick Thomas, "The Pay Is High and Jobs Are Plentiful, But Few Want to Go Into Sales," *Wall Street Journal*, July 14, 2021.

Third-Party Data

One way you make your insights unassailable is by using a fact-based, data-driven approach to providing your insights. Your One-Down client might want to argue with you and reject your perspective, but they are going to find it more difficult to argue with the U.S. Census Bureau, the Federal Reserve's *Beige Book*, the Bureau of Labor Statistics, Gartner, Forrester, the *New York Times*, the *Wall Street Journal*, or Gallup. You can also add internal data from your company, and any internal polls or surveys that your company conducts. Data and facts are more difficult to argue with, especially when they come from multiple sources. My personal approach to being One-Up is to use a good deal of third-party data because it removes any criticism that the data is biased.

Buying Process Insights

One of the major power sources of your One-Up approach is your buying process insights, the Vantage Point strategy. As I explained in Chapter 6, your experience helping your clients change and improve their results provides you with valuable insights. You can then use them to enrich your One-Down clients' judgment about what conversations they need to have and what commitments they need to make to produce the better results they need.

Technical Insights

Not having sold anything with a technical component, I am One-Down with the experience of capturing these insights and using them to support a One-Up approach to selling. However, I know many salespeople and sales organizations with technical offerings where their technical insights are critical to their success. If you sell something technical, you need to identify and organize those insights.

Execution Insights

There are insights you only acquire when you recognize why your clients struggle to produce the results they need. Many of these insights show up in how your client executes. This book is based on the One-Up insight that the legacy approaches to sales are no longer adequate and are the root cause of poor sales results. You might find this idea extends to a lot of industries and companies that are using legacy approaches, while others have updated how they do things.

If You Are Not One-Up You Are One-Down

There is no middle ground between One-Up and One-Down. Either you are One-Up, leading your client because you have greater knowledge and experience with the decisions they need to make and the better results they need, or you are One-Down. Allowing your client to be One-Up is a dereliction of your duty as a professional salesperson, since being One-Down prevents you from creating value for your client in the sales conversation. Letting your client lead means the person who knows less than you and lacks the requisite experience is determining how to improve their own results, making you irrelevant.

The path to being One-Up requires that you do the work of building and organizing your insights into a perspective that helps your clients change their beliefs.

8

One-Up Guide to Offering Advice and Recommendations

In giving advice seek to help, not to please your friend.

—Solon

I WAS BORN on the very southern end of One-Down, so far from One-Up that it was a five-hour trip just to get to the wrong side of the tracks. For a long time, I thought that put me at a disadvantage, but I've come to believe that the only lasting adversity is never facing adversity at all—you only grow when you have something to push against. It's better to be born poor and end up rich than it is to be born rich and not learn the habits that prevent you from ending up poor. Flooding Facebook with shots of your big, expensive cars and your gigantic house shows that you're One-Down in a particularly pernicious way: It's proof that money can allow you to look happy when you are suffering inside.

I hate to kick someone when they're One-Down, but to be honest, most salespeople limit their advice and recommendations to "buy my solution from my company." The limit of their help is the amount of value they create for their clients, which in this case is little or none. To be One-Up, your guidance and recommendations must span the entire sales conversation and consistently inform your client's decisions.

Imagine that you are looking for work in the craft we call sales, and you have two job offers on the table. The first offer is from an incredibly successful and well-recognized company. They have an outstanding marketing department, so their products and services are known to all in the market they serve. There is high demand for what this company sells. Accepting this job comes with a good salary and a wonderful commission structure. You will also have big-name clients assigned to you, making it easy to sell.

The second company is successful but does not have the name recognition or high profile of the first one. They have almost no marketing, and they are not yet well-recognized in the market you'd be responsible for selling to. There is significant demand for what this company sells, but because the market has been commoditized, you will have to displace your competition to win deals. The salary is about the same, and the commission plan is also very attractive.

You might be attracted to the first job offer because it sounds easier, and I wouldn't blame you. The second position would be more difficult, especially that part about having to displace your competitors in a commoditized market, rather than just renewing the same set of contracts with the same handful of named clients. But you'd make a significant concession by agreeing to work at the first company: Its seeming advantages would make it far more difficult for you to become One-Up. In fact, you're far more likely to succumb to laziness and end up One-Down.

My most respected peers in sales consulting all learned to sell by selling commodities. Jeb Blount sold uniforms, a service with no differentiation; in some cases, the same manufacturer produced his uniforms and his competitor's. Mike Weinberg sold specialized plastic fittings, among other things, though he'd be unable to explain why his plastic fittings were superior to the competition's. As for me, I sold temporary staffing, competing against companies that provided the very same service with a database that was indistinguishable from my own. One of the challenges of selling in a commoditized market is that your prospective clients already buy what you sell. Your suggestion cannot be that your client should buy your solution; they've already taken that advice—from your competitor, no less. But Jeb, Mike, and I all greatly benefited from not being able to rely on our company or our solutions to create any real, tangible (or intangible, for that matter) differentiation. Instead, we had to differentiate by providing a different level of advice and recommendations about how our clients should make decisions for their businesses.

Make no mistake: You should eventually advise your client to buy what you sell from your company; after all, you are a professional salesperson! But only after you offer all kinds of other, arguably more important, advice and recommendations. In short, to earn the right to pitch your product, you must first become truly consultative.

Things to Consider When Providing Advice

Before we can fully explore the strategies for providing consultative advice and recommendations, we need to address two primary obstacles that prevent salespeople from offering guidance outside of *buy from me*. Removing these obstacles will better equip you to provide the guidance your client needs. It's also important to understand when it's *not* a good idea to give advice. Let's start with the obstacles.

Obstacles

The first obstacle is the belief that you shouldn't offer advice outside of what you sell. When your knowledge enables your client to produce a better outcome for their company or their clients, being One-Up obligates you to share your advice. It's important to recognize that if your client were already doing what they needed to do to produce better results, they wouldn't need your advice—they'd already be generating better results.

The second obstacle to advising your clients is the belief that your client knows more than you and is better positioned to decide. Perhaps you think they're One-Up based on their title, the amount of time they have been in business, their level of success, or some other factor. The fact that they've asked for your assistance trumps all of that. If they already knew everything they needed to know about this decision, they wouldn't be sitting in front of you expecting you to provide them with help.

A short definition of consultative sales is "the act of helping someone create a result they were unable to achieve without the salesperson's counsel." Your advice and the actions you prescribe are a part of how you help your contacts to correct their course and create the results they need.

When Not to Give Advice

There are going to be times when you should not advise your prospective client. On occasion, you might be One-Up in several areas that would be helpful to the people and companies you serve while being completely and entirely One-Down in another area where they need help. When you are One-Down, meaning you lack the knowledge and experience to provide good counsel, the best approach is to refer your client to a One-Up friend or colleague who can help. It's a good practice to develop relationships with people who are One-Up in other fields for just this purpose, because it allows you continue to create value for your client when what they need lies outside your expertise.

One of the side effects of being One-Up is that occasionally people will ask you for advice in areas where you have no experience and little knowledge. When you have a relationship with a client, it is not uncommon for them to share other, more personal challenges, mistaking your One-Upness in one area as proof that you are One-Up in other areas. Commercial relationships are still relationships, but it is always a mistake to provide advice in areas where you lack expertise, especially when it's personal. You can always listen, empathize, and help guide them to someone who actually is One-Up and can help them sort things out. When you are One-Down, all you have to offer is an opinion, and you should avoid offering opinions in areas outside of your specialty.

How to Teach Your Prospective Clients to Take Your Advice

There is no reason for you to withhold your advice and recommendations until you physically (or even virtually) step into your dream client's office. You can start this process far earlier than you might think, capturing the mindshare necessary to be known as being One-Up and a potential strategic partner. Let's say you print an article that explains some part of the client's world to them, highlight what's important, and include a note about why you believe your client should care. By reading the article and your notes or highlights, your client has already started taking your advice. This is a perfect first step in helping them learn to take your advice, demonstrating that you are willing and able to help them improve their position.

A modern, insight-based approach to selling starts with communication designed to give your contacts valuable information and insights—the same kind of content that might make up your executive briefing, even if it's not as complete. If you avoid pairing this data with a sales pitch, this approach also positions you as someone known for their ideas, their advice, and their suggestions. I need to caution you here about how you communicate as a One-Up salesperson. The reason I don't believe that you should prospect through email, especially not using fully automated sequences, is that it trains your prospect to ignore your emails. You want your client to be excited about reading your emails because what you send is always valuable to them. The good news is that most of your competition will use email and other One-Down, conflict-averse, asynchronous mediums that will all but guarantee they'll never be a threat to you.

Another way to teach your clients to take your advice is to make your recommendations valuable to them. This starts with how you approach the very first sales conversation. In Chapter 2, we discussed how you might make a sales call without mentioning your company, clients, or solutions; without trying to build rapport; and without asking your prospective client to disclose the source of their dissatisfaction. To execute the One-Up approach through your advice and your recommendations, you must eliminate your strong inclination to push your product or solution early in the sales conversation. There's a time and a place for that material, typically at the end of your presentation and proposal. By clearing that deadweight from your early interactions, you make room for advice in a dozen other areas—where your recommendations will create real value for the decision-makers and decision-shapers you serve.

In the sales conversation, you demonstrate that you are the right person to work with by skillfully facilitating your buyer's journey, causing your client to recognize that they have gained something from every conversation. You employ that same strategy by making recommendations that serve your prospects—even if they never buy from you. In fact, here's a good accountability test: "Would my advice still be true if my competitor gave it?" If your advice is sound regardless of its source, then you can be certain it's valuable. However you use your knowledge, your experience, and your One-Up strategies and tactics, your goal is to help your contacts see their problems with new eyes, recognize the path to better results, and weigh the factors relevant to their decision. As it pertains to the buyer's journey and your sales conversation, you need to provide good counsel outside of what you sell.

Giving Advice: Two Tactics

Now that you have a better idea of what sort of advice to offer, here are two tactics for working that advice into your conversations. Play with both of them to get your scripts right and find natural transitions into the advice or recommendation.

1. **Ask for permission.** One way you might approach offering your advice and recommendations is to ask for permission when it is not necessary. You might say something like, "Would it be okay if I shared with you what seems to be the most valuable next step and produces the best overall long-term results?"

You'll notice that this is frequently part of the soft-approach examples in the next section. Asking for permission, especially permission to share, often prompts your contacts to give you their attention long enough for you to explain the value of the next step, along with the negative consequences they are certain to incur if they avoid what they need to do. It also does a great deal of work to move a large ego out of the way, especially with a contact who is used to driving. You are letting them keep their hands on the wheel even though you are navigating.

2. **Tell the client what to do.** The other way you can offer your contacts advice and recommendations is by directly telling them what they should do next, to move them forward toward the better future results they need. It sounds like this: "I'll schedule a meeting to bring our operations team to meet with your operations team, to make sure we have a deep understanding of what they are going to need from us." To get to this point, it can help to ask a question designed to expose One-Down behavior. That helps the client understand why you're telling them to do something.

Whether you ask for permission or take charge, do your best to make your advice and recommendations seem natural. Your primary goal here is to prevent your client from making mistakes that will harm their results.

The Advice and Recommendations You Must Provide

The need to provide advice across all sorts of areas is one our profession rarely recognizes. It's a One-Up observation outside the ken of the legacy approaches to sales. The reason your clients need your help in many different areas is because they can't solve their *presenting problem* until they can address their deeper, problem-solving problems. On the rare occasions that One-Down salespeople even recognize their clients' problem-solving problems, they are ill-equipped to do anything about it, often falling into a vicious cycle of One-Downness. In the remainder of this section you will find several categories of advice, to help you advise your clients in broader, more meaningful, and much more helpful ways. For each category, I've included two types of sample language: a soft/diplomatic approach and a tougher one that exposes One-Down behavior.

How Best to Pursue Change

This first piece of advice comes from your vantage point (Chapter 6). Because you have made dozens, hundreds, or (for my fellow venerable salespeople) thousands of sales calls, you know what conversations your clients need to have to successfully pursue the outcomes you helped them recognize. Because you are One-Up, you should be leading the client by recommending the next step you take together.

Soft approach: "Can I share with you something you might consider as a first step? It might help you explore an idea that will be really valuable as you start to consider doing something different."

Exposing One-Down behavior: "When our other clients skip this part of the conversation, they have struggled to move forward. Is it worth taking the time to do this in the right order, instead of having to start over later?"

Who to Include

This is another vantage-point insight that translates into powerful advice for your client. You may find yourself staring down a contact who is overconfident about their own power, insisting that they do not need to include stakeholders who are going to be affected by a decision to change. You might also find your main contact does not believe that their change initiative will need an executive sponsor (one who co-controls the company's checkbook). When you recognize that your conversation is missing people with titles or roles that are always part of the process, you must address that gap with a recommendation. Your support needs to help your client bring the necessary people into the conversation, even if it's sooner than they expect, if they want to make change.

Soft approach: "One of the risks here is getting so far out in front of your team that they might resist any change because they have been left out of the conversation. How do we bring them into this conversation so they can stay on track with us and create the buy-in that will be necessary later?"

Exposing One-Down behavior: "How do we prevent your team from resisting buy-in or a new approach? They might claim to have the moral high ground if they are excluded from the decision."

Changing Priorities and Goals

One of the benefits of being One-Up is helping your clients change their priorities. You might find your client prioritizing an outcome that they should be pursuing after they complete a different change initiative. In the different worlds where I have offered advice, for example, I have counseled clients to prioritize retention over attraction when it came to their hiring priorities. I have also advised sales organizations to train their sales managers before they train their entire sales force, since the managers will have to execute the necessary changes in beliefs and behaviors.

Soft approach: "Can I offer you a suggestion about the order in which you pursue these goals and why the sequence here matters?"

Exposing One-Down behavior: "Is it better to do the first initiative first, even if it takes a little longer to get started, so we
can speed up future initiatives and start generating the best
results sooner?"

Event Timing

It is common for decision-makers and other stakeholders to have
some conversations in the wrong order. For example, you may have
an incredibly powerful discovery meeting, and your client immediately wants you to send them a proposal and pricing. You don't
need to be reminded that sending either one would be premature
at best and a deal killer at worst. Your counsel needs to ensure that
you help your client get the right conversations in the right order.

Soft approach: "I would love to give you a proposal, but I am
afraid that without dialing in our approach with your team,
it's not going to be right. Can I recommend a couple meetings
we might have to ensure you get exactly what you need?"

Exposing One-Down behavior: "I know that you already see
what you need to do. How do we make sure what we've been
discussing is right for all the other people who are going to
weigh in later?"

Improving Competitiveness

It is not uncommon for prospective clients to think they're doing
just fine without your help. Your experience and One-Up expertise tell you otherwise. You might advise your client to let you
do an analysis on their business, so you can provide them with
recommendations that might help them do even better. With
a simple and relatively crude maturity model, you can provide
instruction and a road map to show them how they can go from
lagging to good enough to competitive to best in class. You can

also just provide the maturity model and the direction it recommends without asking to do a full analysis.

Soft approach: "You are perfectly positioned for some quick wins by making two changes to what you are doing now. Can I show you why you might make those changes and how you might go about doing so?"

Exposing One-Down behavior: "How important is it to you and your business to have a competitive advantage in your market? Would you make changes if they would provide you with a greater ability to compete and win?"

What Problem They Should Solve

At this point, it's important to notice that none of your advice involves buying anything from you: it's about solving problems more effectively. Sometimes that means choosing the right problem to solve. For example, one day a good friend called me and told me that his team was terrible at presenting and negotiating. His evidence? His team lost almost every deal they pursued. He believed the presenting problem—their poor presentation and negotiation skills—was the root cause of their losses. Four questions later, he told me that one hundred percent of their deals came from RFPs. That prompted a much different, and much more fruitful, conversation about how they pursued opportunity capture.

Soft approach: "I understand that you need to solve this problem. What I am afraid of is that without first resolving the larger problem that is the root cause, you are not going to produce the results you could. What do you think?"

Exposing One-Down behavior: "How much of an impact does the underlying problem contribute to this problem, and do you believe it's possible to improve your results without addressing that root cause?"

Recommend and Replace Poor Beliefs

In Chapter 5 you learned that your clients often hold false assumptions, make mistakes, and underestimate the implications of their changing world until it's too late. Even though you may not advise the client directly to change their beliefs, recommending a better and more complete view of their world through your insights is critical to change.

Soft approach: "There is a lot of new data that has not gotten the attention it should have. Can I show you what's changed and what it suggests about any future decisions you might make?"

Exposing One-Down behavior: "There is a lot of new data you need to pay attention to. Can I show you what's changed to see how this is tracking with your experience?"

Change Their Metrics

When a company or a stakeholder leans heavily on a particular metric, it's not unusual for them to treat that measurement as sacrosanct. For example, you might need to advise your client to switch their primary metric from profitability on a transaction to the lifetime value of the client. The change is powerful if it reveals that your client could invest more in acquiring new clients based on their lifetime profitability.

Soft approach: "That metric is important, but it doesn't always show you the whole picture. One of our recommendations is that you use that metric in conjunction with this additional metric, because it provides a more complete view and opens up new potential."

Exposing One-Down behavior: "If there were a metric that provided you greater clarity on your results and your future decisions, would you want your team to track that metric in addition to the ones you use now?"

Change a Business Process

Sometimes your advice needs to address an archaic process that has outlived its effectiveness. When a critical process a client uses no longer serves them, you recommend its replacement—even when it isn't something that you sell.

When HubSpot cold-called me, for instance, the salesperson began our conversation by establishing himself as One-Up. He suggested that my strategy for growing my newsletter was awful and that there were several core strategies I was not using. Within 10 minutes, I learned a few things I did not know about newsletter promotion, releasing me from being One-Down. I later changed my process based on the salesperson's advice.

The soft language the salesperson used to get me to engage in changing a process was, "We can see that you are trying to grow your newsletter, but we'd have you do something different that would increase your signups. Can we share our ideas with you?"

Naturally, I agreed to hear him out.

Factors to Consider

You are trying to create value for your clients, largely by leveraging your insights, your knowledge, and your experience. These things combine to provide you a perspective on what's important for your clients as it pertains to their decisions. Specifically, you will evaluate the factors your client needs to consider and how they should weigh them. Because the list is inexhaustible, we'll touch on a few common factors, knowing you will have to create a more specific list that you can share with your clients. Remember, you are teaching your client what they need to know to make the best decision for their company, creating a greater level of value than your legacy approach competitors can provide. How could a person who has been converted from One-Down to One-Up not want to work with the person who shaped the decision for them?

Soft approach: "Which of these factors is most important to you now, and could you prioritize a different factor if it led to better results faster?"

Exposing One-Down behavior: "Up until now, that factor was most important to your results. It no longer holds that rank, even though it's still important. Are you open to exploring which factors contribute more now?"

What Delivery Model Best Suits Them

Every company has a delivery model they believe provides them with an advantage. These models live on a continuum, ranging from low-priced transactional models to high-priced strategic partner models. The high-priced models typically offer a high-trust, high-value, and high-caring approach to delivering results. In the muddy middle, there are always several "good enough" competitors who have a higher price than the low-end players and a lower price than the high-end players.

Soft approach: "Would it make sense to pay a higher price if it delivered a lower overall cost by improving your results?"

Exposing One-Down behavior: "Have you done an analysis on what the concessions you are making will do to your overall cost structure?"

One advantage you have here is that your competitors never list out all the concessions their (cheaper) models require, so your client is usually unaware what they are agreeing to accept. But be cautious: If the evidence suggests they need a delivery model you don't sell, pushing your model anyway forfeits your One-Up status.

Increase Their Investment

The world of B2B invariably features clients who want to reduce the investment they make in the results they need. In the long history of our Universe, there has never been an outcome that was improved by investing less time and energy. There is, however, unlimited and unassailable evidence that boosting both investments improves results the way nothing else can. Much of the time, the advice you need to offer your prospective clients is to invest more.

Soft approach: "The investment you are making now is no longer enough to produce the results you need. This is true no matter who you choose as a partner. Can I share with you the areas many in our space avoid investing in to avoid the problems you have now?"

Exposing One-Down behavior: "I don't want you to underinvest in the results you need, because that will cost you more over time and give you a new set of problems. No matter who you choose, and no matter what they say, you need to invest more, not less."

When you offer your advice about what your client needs, what you say needs to be true no matter who delivers the solution. You are not proposing your solution yet, but you are helping your client design the solution they will eventually need. This is how you position what you sell to fit your client's needs.

The Trading Value Rule

Every time you give advice or recommendations, you should follow the trading value rule: Explain exactly how your client is going to benefit from taking your advice or following your recommendations—even if they never buy from you. (But don't worry; they are going to buy from you.)

The reason you can offer any advice at all is because you are One-Up. Your experience gives you all the evidence you need to be certain that your counsel will benefit your contacts. Your client is One-Down because they don't yet know that they are going to find your counsel incredibly valuable. To take full advantage of that gap, you must explain how what you are asking them to do advances them toward the better future state to which you are guiding them.

You should also be prepared for your client to express concerns about what you ask them to do. Human beings tend to bring up lesser fears when they don't want to engage big ones. Your recommendation that your client should bring an executive sponsor to the next meeting may elicit anxiety that they aren't prepared to make their case this early to an executive. That concern is real, and you should do the work to ensure that your contact can and will acquire the executive's support. But the bigger risk, one you and your client both need to address, is getting so far out in front of the executive that, for whatever reason, they can't or won't support the initiative. Maybe the time you and your contact lost allowed another person on the executive's team to propose another important initiative. Or perhaps, having been left out of the "why change" conversation, the executive does not recognize the initiative's importance.

You might worry that providing your client with the information they need to be One-Up will prevent them from needing your help, let alone paying you for it. To create value for your contact, you must help remove them from being One-Down and make them One-Up. Their One-Upness will be no match for yours; no matter how much you've taught them, they can't equal your insights and your experience. But they'll still be One-Up compared to the rest of their team.

You taught them everything they know, but you did not teach them everything you know. It is highly unlikely that you could teach your clients all that you know, even if you wanted to.

Because so much expertise operates at the subconscious level, you don't know everything you know. Your subconscious is skilled at pattern recognition, which is how you recognize your client's problem about five minutes after your contact starts talking.

One of the outcomes of being One-Up is that your client begins to depend on you to help them make important decisions. Once they know that you are going to cover a particular area for them, they release that responsibility to you, confident that you are going to keep them abreast of anything that needs or deserves their attention. Those who lack the depth and the intellectual curiosity to continue to build out their insights and organize their experience will disappoint a client who believes they've got an expert paying attention for them.

9

The One-Up Obligation
to Proactively Compel Change

Do not wait to strike until the iron is hot; but make it hot by striking.
—*William B. Sprague*

MY TIME SELLING what many consider a commodity really sharpened my already competitive nature. There are two major challenges when you sell a commodity. First, every client you call on already has a provider for what you sell. Second, most of your clients are not yet compelled to change, the one element you need to create and win a deal. Recently, I read that only three percent of any market is actually pursuing a change at any time, a figure that matches my own experience, at least in some industries.

When confronted by these two deeply intertwined challenges, a lot of salespeople wonder whether they should instead try to target the companies that are not already buying whatever it is they sell. Unless you have something that is going to make its own market, there is little reason ever to call on a company that does not need what you sell. When you live in the red ocean, you might dream of blue water, unstained by the blood of those who find themselves on the losing end of a contest. But in reality, many markets are dominated by competitive displacement sales, where each salesperson must remove their competition to win a client. The primary challenge in this type of sale is not that your client already has a provider. It's the fact that they are not compelled to change.

Problems don't age well. They tend to metastasize, growing in size and spreading throughout an organization. The longer a company avoids tackling a problem, the more they learn to live with it, eventually accepting that *this is just how it is*. As a result, companies are often forced to change on a timeline outside their control, causing them to rush the decision to change, make mistakes, and be unable to execute their new methods or initiatives. One of the reasons the traditional discovery call has weakened over time is that a complex environment makes avoiding change attractive, especially when the change comes with risk, conflict,

159

and an increase in uncertainty. Unfortunately, many salespeople still believe that *identifying a problem* and finding the client's *pain point* is all that is necessary to compel change. But clients don't avoid change because they're ignorant of their problems. They avoid it because the prospect of changing is about as appealing as a simultaneous quadruple bypass, craniectomy, and root canal.

Your One-Up approach must include the ability to proactively help your clients change, perhaps the most difficult sales task in a complex environment. This is not just good business: As a One-Up salesperson, you have an ethical obligation to help your clients change before events force them to do so.

The fact that you are One-Up requires that you remove your clients from their One-Down position, in this case by helping them proactively change to avoid harm. To do otherwise is to shirk your duty—a responsibility that is difficult, time-consuming, and sometimes frustrating, but at the same time the most meaningful and purposeful work you can do in sales. Few deals are more satisfying than the ones where you recognize a problem and help your client avoid it, despite the legacy (and One-Down) belief that it's better to solve the problem after your client's already been hurt.

Proactive work is rarely easy or simple, making it a good litmus test of your commitment to being One-Up. But here's the good news: because you are One-Up, your vantage point, your ability to provide a better experience of the sales conversation, and your insights all position you to compel change—while also providing the confidence and certainty that you can help your change-averse clients to move forward before they are harmed.

The State of Uncertainty in the Sales Sequence

Change follows a subtle but consistent pattern, which I call the certainty sequence: Uncertainty → Certainty of Negative Consequences (Threshold) → Uncertainty → Certainty of Positive Outcomes. The pattern provides you with a guide to creating and winning new opportunities, however, most people get the pattern backward. Despite this, sometimes it's necessary to follow the right sequence, something we don't pay nearly enough attention to as we go about our work helping our prospects and clients manage change.

Much of the time, you find your contacts in a state of uncertainty. They know they have problems, which is why you don't need to bludgeon them with questions to extract a full confession. The complex environment they exist within is extremely difficult to understand, making it challenging to know what to do and when to do it. Decision-makers who pay attention to the news to stay abreast of their environment and improve their decisions often end up with greater uncertainty. They consider questions like: Is the economy going to grow or shrink? Is my industry going to be saddled with new legislation that will change my profit margin? Where is our next competitive threat coming from? Are we going to be able to overcome it?

In legacy approaches, salespeople create slide decks that attempt to generate certainty. They show that your company is a good company with great products and services, and a lot of big-name clients. You might even believe that your role as a consultative salesperson is to move your client directly from uncertainty to certainty, but you would be wrong. None of your slides can create certainty because you are violating the sequence. Before you can create certainty that you can help your client reach positive outcomes, you first need to move through two other stages.

Certainty of Negative Consequences

Before creating optimistic certainty, you need to create certainty that your prospective client will suffer the negative consequences if they maintain the status quo and wait too long to address their challenges. You must help them realize that they cannot wait too long to address their challenges. By not changing, they are sure to face more difficult and expensive problems later.

The way we used to think about discovery would have you ask your client to tell you about their problems, so you can gain the information you believe you need to help your client. A more modern and robust version of discovery has you help your client identify what they need to learn to move forward. In this stage, they need to be certain that they will experience increasingly negative consequences until they change. You can call this *the threshold*, the state in which your contacts are motivated to change. John Kotter, a leadership professor at Harvard Business School, would describe this as a burning platform, the urgency to act.

You may not *want* your client to shift from feeling certain doom to once again feeling uncertainty, but that is exactly where the certainty sequence takes them next. And there's a good reason for that.

Back to Uncertainty: The Need to Change

Confronted with the urgent need to change, the client will again feel uncertain. At this stage, their uncertainty comes from the prospect of making a decision in a complex and uncertain environment. These are the problems that prevent clients from solving their problems—and they're the domain of consultative salespeople.

Your contacts are uncertain about the choices they have, how to best address their challenges, and whether their organization will successfully implement the change. These fears make it even harder for clients to change because they are also uncertain about whether changing will make things worse. Here, a consultative approach is necessary to move decision-makers and decision-shapers to the certainty they need to move forward.

Certainty of Positive Outcomes

To enable your contacts to make a decision and move forward with a new initiative, you have to provide certainty of positive outcomes. To do this, you design a plan clients believe they can execute, build consensus, address budget issues, and resolve all the concerns that would prevent your prospective client from reaching the better results they need. A slide deck alone cannot solve any of these issues. Instead, they require real conversations, with individuals and groups working together to build certainty.

The sales conversation is a dynamic interaction, one more like a Rubik's Cube than a linear process or buyer's journey. You can use your slide deck to create a sliver of certainty as you open discovery calls and presentations, but the only reliable path comes from creating value for your client throughout the sales conversation.

Unaddressed Uncertainty in Legacy Sales

Much of what we get wrong here is the order of the sales conversation. As much as marketers want you to tell your company's story and share your CEO's bona fides, that does nothing to address your clients' uncertainty in any meaningful way. The product manager would want you to share the tremendous advantages of your product or your service. This approach also leaves the uncertainty unaddressed.

The real outcome missing from the legacy approaches to discovery is compelling change in a complex world. This explains why the problem–pain–solution pattern is increasingly losing its efficacy. More deals than ever end without a decision, and the fact that 70 percent of all B2B change initiatives end in failure, with only 5 percent meeting their objectives, isn't making it easier to help clients change.[1]

---

[1] Taylor Landis, "Customer Retention Marketing vs. Customer Acquisition Marketing," OutboundEngine, April 20, 2021.

Each conversation you have with a client should help move them through the certainty sequence, with the ultimate goal of creating enough certainty to execute a change initiative. To do that, you must recognize what type of certainty your client needs to move forward toward a better future state.

Why Clients Resist Change

Few scholars have thought as much about large-scale organizational change as John Kotter. His book *Leading Change* was an international bestseller, and the sequel, *The Heart of Change*, is even more accessible and actionable. Kotter's change framework includes eight steps, but here we're going to focus on the first one: creating a sense of urgency.

Specifically, Kotter writes, "those who are most successful at significant change begin their work by creating a sense of urgency among relevant people." According to Kotter, the population of relevant people is far larger than we might expect: close to 100 in small companies, and likely close to 1000 in larger companies. Change leaders fail, Kotter notes, because they "aim at 5 or 50 or 0, allowing what is common nearly everywhere—too much complacency, fear, or anger, all three of which can undermine change. A sense of urgency, sometimes developed by very creative means, gets people off the couch, out of a bunker, and ready to move."[2] You have already learned one of Kotter's core effective methods in Chapter 3, something he describes as "see, feel, change." In his words, "[c]ompelling, eye-catching, dramatic situations are created to help others visualize problems, solutions, or progress in solving complacency, strategy, empowerment, or other key problems within the eight steps."

---

[2] John P. Kotter, *The Heart of Change: Real-Life Stories of How People Change Their Organizations* (Boston: Harvard Business Review Press, 2002), 3.

Creating Certainty to Compel Change

Later in this book, we'll explore how to create the certainty necessary to move forward with change. A lot of sales organizations view certainty only in terms of getting their clients to sign a contract, take delivery, and move forward with a new "solution." This is a One-Down approach, as it assumes that the client isn't changing because they are uncertain about the sales company's ability to help them improve their results. This belief is incorrect. While it's true your client needs certainty to move forward, the certainty they need isn't about you, your company, or your solution; it's about the inevitable negative consequences of maintaining the status quo for so long that their results suffer and threaten their business.

In one sales call, I worked incredibly hard to help a client recognize that their plan would fail them in the third quarter of that year. He was one of those people who knows everything and expects the salesperson to act like a One-Down vendor, someone who needs the client's business more than the client needs the help. I disappointed him. Having shown him the data, I explained how far off his assumptions were from reality, but he was unmoved. I am not particularly proud of my last-ditch effort to change his mind after spending 90 minutes trying to prevent a future disaster. I said, "In September, you are going need a shovel and plot to bury your business. I want you to know that you will be shutting down your lines. Please speak to other people in our space who will tell you this is true." He said that he would take his chances.

I failed this client, and in September, he asked his team to call me and see if we could help get his lines running without their making the changes I had advised. I declined, and a year later, his strong commitment to avoiding a necessary decision cost him all his clients. He didn't have to lose his clients or his business, but it was more important for him to believe that I was wrong about the consequences. Here is the point: To compel change, you have to create the certainty of future negative consequences.

If there is no certainty that something wicked this way comes, your prospective client can, and most likely will, avoid change.

You know what the negative consequences are when a client refuses to make a necessary change until their results start to suffer. One of the things that makes you One-Up is your ability to predict the future, something that is easy to do because you meet with clients every day who are already struggling because they have waited too long to change. A list of all the reasons that your prospective clients change is all you need to identify the things that should be compelling them to change. But there are also certain concerns that compel change that cannot be addressed directly without harming your approach.

Our Immunity to Change

Gary Klein has already provided us with the insight that people's beliefs create anchors, preventing them from changing until they have their false assumptions replaced. We can supplement this perspective with the work of Robert Kegan and Lisa Laskow Lahey, who co-authored *Immunity to Change: How to Overcome It and Unlock the Potential in Yourself and Your Organization*. Here's how they talk about complexity and change:

> When we experience the world as "too complex," we are not just experiencing the complexity of the world. We are experiencing a mismatch between the world's complexity *and our own this moment*. There are only two logical ways to mend this mismatch—reduce the world's complexity or increase our own. The first isn't going to happen. The second has long seemed an impossibility in adulthood.[3]

---

[3] Robert Kegan and Lia Laskow Lahey, *Immunity to Change: How to Overcome It and Unlock the Potential in Yourself and Your Organization* (Boston: Harvard Business Press, 2009), 12.

Indeed, we usually find our clients amid an ongoing, frustrating dilemma, but they've often been in that state so long that they've accepted it. While they should be compelled to change, especially when they care about the problem deeply, they haven't yet addressed the source of their frustration. By providing One-Up insights, advice, and recommendations, you can help expand the limits of your client's understanding, especially in terms of knowing how to change.

The final element of optimal conflict is support so clients feel, to use Kegan and Lahey's words, "neither overwhelmed by the conflict nor able to escape or diffuse it."[4] You are perfectly equipped as a One-Up salesperson to provide the necessary support to lead change. Many of the pieces are already in place. You now know that your insights can correct the information disparity that causes your client to feel as if their problems exceed their current knowledge of the world, and their way of understanding it. You also know that your updated discovery call is going to help your client discover something about themselves, something you enable by telling them a story that makes sense of their world by providing a higher-resolution lens. Because you have helped your other clients improve their results through your advice and your recommendations, your vantage point provides a way forward.

There are other challenges that you must dispatch to compel your client to change, some of which are difficult to overcome. Kegan and Lahey identify the root causes that prevent change as unconscious commitments that are in conflict and based on major assumptions. To address these obstacles to change, we have to look at them through a lens suited to the work of the One-Up sale. In our world we often talk about *objections*, a word that is not accurate for complex B2B environments. So let's reframe and redefine objections, replacing them with a number of challenges that more accurately define what prevents change.

---

[4] Ibid.

Individual Immunities Expressed as Objections

By illuminating the nature of change, we can learn something about ourselves and gain an advantage when it comes to helping our clients change. The most important work you can do to improve your results in sales is to improve your understanding of human beings and how they operate. By studying both sales and psychology (this book tries to check both boxes), you can observe what people project about themselves in ways they may not even realize.

You'll encounter a number of immunities to change whenever you try to compel it. Some people think that humans are basically rational but are prone to being emotional from time to time. But the truth is quite the opposite: we are inherently emotional and rationalize our decisions to align them with much deeper needs. These needs are what Kegan and Lahey call "hidden commitments," the things that drive an immunity to change when left unaddressed. Kegan and Lahey get granular because they deal with individuals who participate in a process that includes their team, but we're going to look at broader (and relatively more visible) forces.

This section aims to illuminate things invisible to most others. The lens we will look through will also help us recognize something about ourselves, and in doing so, provide an advantage when it comes to helping clients change. You must look at people and what they project about themselves, even subconsciously. The most important work you can do to improve your results in sales is to improve your understanding of humans and how they operate. You are better off reading books about psychology than books about sales (with a few rare exceptions, this book being one of them!).

Kegan and Lahey's work gets granular because they deal with individuals who participate in a team process. For our purposes, we must look at the forces that are easier to see.

- **Position:** The nature of our work in sales puts us in contact with individuals pursuing position, a place higher up the hierarchy. Position provides power, or a proximity to power, and the rewards that come with position. An individual may refuse any attempt to change if it threatens their position.

- **Purpose:** Some of the same people who once vied for position often seek something that will leave a lasting impact, a legacy. It's now common to find more people motivated by making a positive difference, regardless of their age or their role. It's not uncommon for individuals to resist or disengage from change that works against their purpose and values.

- **Transformation:** Some stakeholders you encounter will be natural-born change-makers, pursuing their own transformation and trying to drag others along with them. They resist anything that isn't transformational enough to pique their interest. Some will join those who instigate change when it serves their needs.

- **Risk Aversion:** This type of person worries that any change will cause even greater problems or challenges. They often play the devil's advocate unless a change initiative can be shown to reduce risk.

- **Inclusion:** Some people need to belong to a group; others fear exclusion from the group. This driving force can cause someone to support a change if it means being part of a larger group. However, they may oppose any change that might cause the group to reject or ostracize them.

- **Novelty:** Some percentages of humans are easily bored and require new experiences. They always want to know what comes next, so their immunity prevents any interest in what they perceive to be "more of the same."

■ **Survival:** Survival can create the strongest immunity to change, especially when someone is already under threat of some negative outcome or consequence. Survival is a desperate place, causing a person to do whatever is necessary to endure.

You have to recognize the forces that either compel or prevent change, and then you need to tailor your interactions to meet their needs. For example, if someone values inclusion or novelty, you will struggle to create certainty by appealing to their position or personal significance. You don't ask a contact directly how a new initiative will threaten their position and their rewards. Instead, you have to pay attention to what you hear and perceive in meetings. The evidence is available for those who seek it. It's also important that you recognize the overlap in these immunities, because they are contextual. Any individual (yourself included) occupies any one of these states. The reason gossip exists is because it allows people to share the things that flesh out others' characters and motivations, providing direction on how to best interact with them.

A timed-well, matter-of-fact question can expose an individual's hidden immunities, even when they are difficult to discern. For example: "What does John need to support this initiative?"

This simple approach provides people with what they already need and avoids anything that threatens their goals and their needs. When what you propose causes someone to lose their position, you can expect them to refuse to support the change. A person who is risk averse will always have unresolved concerns, not because you didn't do enough to resolve them, but because it is their nature, and perhaps their role in their company.

You will not remove this immunity to change by sharing how much the shareholders will value your change initiative. You will do better to speak to how it makes a difference.

One challenge of recognizing the needs of others is that our own experiences give us a type of myopia that prevents us from seeing things that are further away and harder to see. The best advice for learning how to see things from another perspective is to first understand what your needs are and how you meet them. Then, without saying anything, try to discern the needs of the people you know well by observing them. But there is more to understanding how to see and address the hidden immunities. Stephen Covey taught me the power of being proactive in his landmark book, *The Seven Habits of Highly Effective People*. In that book, he wrote that each of us has an emotional bank account. Covey warned against making a withdrawal from your deposits. Here, I offer what I hope is a modest improvement to Covey's work by combining it with the idea that the deposit should be in the currency that the person prefers, the one that speaks to their deepest needs.

Your clients will understand the rational reason they may need to change, but that won't always overpower the emotional forces that make people immune to change. These are often hidden—from themselves and others.

Urgently Pursuing Urgency

There may be no greater tool for improving your sales effectiveness than creating a sense of urgency. Most attempts to compel change fail because your client has lived with their problem long enough that changing in September feels no different than changing the following January, even when the client will benefit from changing sooner. When your client is more afraid of change than the negative consequences they will experience if they don't change, you have to help them recognize the greater danger.

What makes compelling change so difficult is that you can inadvertently cause your client to believe that your motivation is self-oriented and self-interested. They might perceive that you want them to act now just so you can get ink on paper (and commission check in wallet). You are going to need a One-Up strategy for compelling change that isn't going to undo the good, value-creating work you've done up to this point. If there are no consequences for doing nothing, then there is no reason to be compelled to change.

Addressing Negative Consequences

When your client is already experiencing negative consequences because they have avoided making the changes that would improve their results, you have to speak to those negative outcomes. You can arm yourself for this task by asking a series of data-gathering questions earlier in the sales conversation. Several categories of information will be helpful to both you and your clients when it comes to compelling change.

The first question you might ask is: "How much does this problem cost you in lost revenue, profit, time, clients, and rework?" By asking this question early in the conversation, you can adjust the cost by accounting for the time you spend developing the change initiative. A relatively small loss of $7,000 a week becomes $140,000 during the five months between September and January.

Here's another question that can create value for your client by helping them act sooner rather than later: "What impact is this having on your team?" Working for leaders who aren't solving problems for and with their team can destroy morale, increase turnover, and ruin what might otherwise be a healthy team culture. Like the question before, you want to ask this before you get to the point where your client tells you they are going to kick the can down the road a bit.

Third, try asking, "What has prevented you from making this change in the past, and what will we need to do to prepare your team to tackle this before it becomes a bigger problem?" You can also ask, "What concerns would you have if you were forced to change on a timeline that was not of your choosing and what problems would you expect?"

You cannot ask these questions when you are deep enough into the sales conversation that your client tells you, "I need to think about it" or "It's not the right time." You might have to help move them forward by recounting the lost revenue, the impact to their team, and the high cost of failing their customers and clients.

In a later chapter, we'll explore how to combine the certainty of negative consequences with the certainty of successfully transforming their results, something necessary to move some clients to act.

Bringing the Future Forward

Human beings seek pleasure and avoid pain. However, for any number of reasons, some have a high tolerance for pain, so negative consequences are just one half of compelling change. You can also ask questions early in the conversation that focus on positive results, allowing you to bring the future forward.

Try this one: "What would it mean to you and your team to reclaim the revenue being lost now?" Note that the language is not blaming the client or their team for the problem. We are not trying to create a need for the client to defend themselves. Naturally, they are going to feel a sense of relief, or something like that.

"How different would your team's day look without fighting these problems and where would you want them to spend their time?" Any answer here is certain to be about how much more productive they are going to be with battling an ongoing challenge.

One more example to make sure you nail this line of questioning: "Would it be worth two hard weeks to get through the learning curve, if at the end of those weeks, you would have eliminated your problem?" The timespan is short enough, and as One-Up salesperson, you engender trust by not being afraid to acknowledge difficulty or adversity.

By combining this with the content in Chapter 11, you will find a strategy that you have never seen—one that will not only help your client, but will allow you to remove your competitors from the playing field without ever saying a word about it.

10

Triangulation Strategy: Helping Clients Decide While Avoiding Competition

The president needed to take a position that not only blended the best of each party's views but also transcended them to constitute a third force in the debate.

—Dick Morris

I RARELY WRITE about politics. In fact, I rid myself of anything partisan after my mentor in law school provided me with some One-Up advice: Instead of worrying about politics and presidents, invest your energy into building the life you want for your family. As it pertains to parties, I am a man without a country. For good or for ill, I have been ungovernable since turning 13 years old, the age at which I decided I would govern myself.

In 1992, then-governor Bill Clinton ran against George H.W. Bush and Ross Perot for the U.S. presidency. Some people suggested that Clinton intended this as a dry run for the highest office in the land, so any accusations about his dalliances with women would be old news for his real run in 1996. Instead, Clinton hired an advisor named Dick Morris to help him win the election, something they accomplished through a little-known framework Morris proposed: triangulation strategy. Shuffle a few letters and you get *strangulation tragedy*, which is how it must have felt to Clinton's opponents. The idea was to position Clinton in a very specific way, one that would make it very difficult for his competition to beat him. Clinton was a lifelong Democrat and ran on their ticket. However, he distanced himself from the Democrats on certain issues, like crime. He was not a Republican, so he also distanced himself from the opposing party, but he gave them credit for ideas popular with women with children. Morris helped Clinton triangulate both parties.

Imagine it this way: Clinton was sitting at the top point of the triangle, looking down at the Democrats in one corner and the Republicans in the other. By moving his position above the playing field, he sought to occupy the moral high ground, positioning himself as the person who could be trusted to do what was right, regardless of party. This strategy helped him win what the media called "soccer moms," a group of swing voters concerned about crime and the safety of their children. The rest, as they say, is history.

Don't worry, that's the end of political talk for the rest of this chapter. But as a One-Up salesperson, you too can occupy a place above the playing field, counseling your client on how they should plan and decide, including the decision of whom to choose as a partner. The strategy is quite powerful because it allows you to triangulate your competition, showing your superiority without alienating your client or looking weak. It also allows you to wipe all of your competitors off the playing field at the very same time, without even naming names.

Sometimes you just bump into an approach that works. I don't recall when I first used this strategy, but I do recall why. I was selling staffing services in a highly commoditized market. Like any reasonably large city, mine had hundreds of competitors. Some were small, including bottom feeders who competed on price alone. Some of these price-oriented companies were dishonest with their clients, omitting information that their clients might have considered deal-breakers. But many were much larger than my company, something that seemed to give them the advantage. At one point, I was competing with two of the largest staffing firms on Earth, so I tried to remove both from my client's consideration. Having worked for one of the companies, I had enough ammunition to take them on directly. While I could have trashed them personally, I knew that it would look like sour grapes to my client. Instead, I trashed their model.

Because I knew the client, and had competed against both firms before, I started by explaining our high-touch, high-caring, high-value approach, suggesting that our medium size allowed us to build a program specific to the client's needs. Next, I reminded them that because we were only a few miles away, any decisions about that program would be made locally, not in another state or even another country. I also shared that large firms required a lot of real estate that did nothing to benefit the client, but their costs were baked into their pricing, along with marketing costs. To take out the bargain basement competitors, I showed how their low prices did not allow them to make the necessary investments in marketing and recruitment to identify and hire a quality workforce.

The whole time, I mentioned no company names. I said nothing negative about their people, and accused no one of anything more than choosing a model that, while excellent for some clients' needs, was inadequate for the client I was talking to. Later, I even said nice things about my competitors, including that I had friends at other firms and that they worked hard, our only disagreements being around the delivery model.

While it will never serve you to speak poorly about an individual competitor, you should explain the different models, the different choices they require, who benefits most from those choices, and who those same choices harm. Attacking a competitor will torpedo your own credibility, but you can easily attack the different models they operate and score points for your understanding and advice.

The Value Continuum

Imagine a value continuum, with a transactional model on the far left and a strategic model that creates much greater value on the far right. To make this easy to understand, let's look at the decision to go out for dinner. On the far left of our value continuum, you find a fast-food restaurant. You would expect it to be cheap, but you would not expect an especially high-quality meal or experience. While you might visit a fast-food place if you just want a quick bite, you can expect to be served with divorce papers if it's your choice for a romantic date night. Moving up one step, you find a fast-casual dining restaurant, the kind with a bar, random sports memorabilia on the walls, and a lot of televisions. While the entrees are better than fast food, they're still nothing special. The fast-casual experience removes the need to cook, and adding televisions is appreciated by people who want to watch sports or news while they eat. Again, probably not the best place for your date-night dinner. The third category is high-end chains, like some steakhouses you find in every major city. They are much more expensive than their alternatives, and the quality is much greater. You might find televisions at the bar, but you won't see them in the dining room. The fourth and final category is high-end independent restaurants with the highest-quality dining experience and high prices, the places already booked solid by the time you try to get a reservation for your anniversary dinner. Back to the steakhouse with you!

Choosing where to go for dinner requires you to look at the context of the decision and the outcomes you need. There is nothing inherently wrong with the value models that different restaurants choose, but the right choice for one occasion is wrong for another. Your company operates on a very similar continuum, where different companies compete by making different choices about how to deliver value in a specific way. Executing the One-Up strategies and tactics you find in this book will help differentiate you as a consultative salesperson, while a triangulation strategy will help position your company as the right partner for your clients by helping them make a more informed and One-Up decision. Every delivery model serves a certain customer with a certain type of need, based on the context of the decision they are making. Sometimes, that means you have to walk away from a potential client, especially the ones trying to achieve better results without making the investments they need. Leave them to your competitors who provide the lowest price, and who often avoid any conversation that might disclose the concessions the client must unknowingly agree to.

I'm sure you'd agree there is no reason to compete for a client who wants high-value results for a no-value investment. But occasionally, a company whose target results require a greater investment mistakenly buys from a company with a pricing model that simply doesn't allow them to produce the results they need. After reading this chapter, you can proactively defend your potential clients from that outcome, massively reducing your odds of losing deals to a low-price competitor.

Singing Their Praises and Confessing Their Sins

In a triangulation strategy, you will sing the praises of each of the competing models, explaining who gains the most value from the model and how it is perfect in a certain context. If you have 20 minutes for lunch between two sales calls, for example, your dining decision will skew toward fast food. You will also confess each model's sins, ensuring your client knows what concessions they are making and how each will harm them. Plowing through McLunch is quick and easy, but the supersized carbs and calories may put you off your game on your second sales call. Every delivery model has an upside and a downside.

Start with the model's positives, explaining why someone would choose that model, but naming no specific competitor. The fact that you will acknowledge the value of the model makes you credible and creates a level of trust, one you would forfeit if you just trashed your competitors, even if everything you said about them was true. You need this trust to confess the model's sins, of which there may be many. You can do this by explaining the concessions the client must make and how the model is wrong when the context of the decision and the desired result don't allow for those concessions. You are an honest broker, sitting next to your client, looking down at the playing field below, and explaining the game to improve your client's understanding of their decisions.

Four Models of Value

To explain how to execute a triangulation model, we have to start by conceptualizing several models, so you can tease apart the differences and teach them to your clients. Our example will use four models, even though you may cover more or fewer in your own conversations. We'll distinguish these models based on the level of value each provides the client, then we'll explore their attributes.

Level One: Commodities—a true commodity, effectively inter-changeable with any similar product

Level Two: Scalable Commodities—also a commodity, but scalable because it provides a better overall experience

Level Three: Solutions—can solve a specific problem by providing a solution and tangible business results

Level Four: Strategic Partners—creates a strategic level of value beyond tangible business results

Commodities

There are a lot of good reasons to buy a commodity, even from a company that will require you to concede to provide you with the lowest price. When there are no negative consequences because of these concessions, there is no reason to make a greater investment. If you walk into a Dollar Tree, you know that you will get the lowest possible price on whatever you buy. But you also know that the experience will not be very good, with overstuffed aisles, difficult-to-reach items, and a rather dismal and somewhat unpleasant environment. However, the staples that you buy there do not differ from what you would pay more for somewhere else.

Whatever your industry, you are certain to come up against competitors who provide a lower price by reducing the investment enough to capture some market share. What's good about these competitors is that they can give clients the lowest price with little friction and the certainty that they are not paying any more than is necessary. What's not so good is that the downside is made up of all kinds of concessions, of which few (if any) are disclosed before the client signs a contract. It's only later that the decision-maker discovers their shipments are always going to be late, that the company offers very little in the way of support or service, and that many of their shipments need to be returned due to the low quality. Triangulating this model requires that you recognize they have the lowest price, show how those prices can benefit the customers for whom the purchase isn't vital, and finally explain the concessions the company makes to deliver the lowest price.

Scalable Commodities

I made up the term *scalable commodity* to describe a delivery model that is one step to the right of outright commodities. A delivery model is one way a company intends to create value and compete for some part of the market. This model corrects for the excesses of the pure commodity by eliminating concessions. It provides greater service and support, improves delivery times, and maybe even eliminates some of the work the customer has to do to manage the relationship. These models have solved the problem of creating a greater level of value on a larger scale, so they often attract clients who find the commodity-model concessions to be untenable.

As you might imagine, even though this model might step toward value, it isn't without its problems. One major concession clients are forced to accept is that these models have systemic problems difficult to resolve, mainly because the companies lack the profit to resolve them completely. Any client who needs consultation and a custom program for their specific outcomes will not find it in a "scalable commodity" delivery model.

Solutions

I detest the word *solution*. I cringe every time I type it because I believe it's past its prime. Instead, we should talk about *outcomes*, which our clients actually want. The first question I ask a client is always: "What outcomes do you need, and why are they important to you now?" You didn't buy this book because you wanted a book; you bought it because you believe it will improve your sales results by improving your approach.

To make this easy to understand, though, let's agree to use the word *solution* to describe the third place on the continuum, again moving left to right. Many companies compete with this delivery model. Its primary value is that it gives the client a solution specifically designed to work for them, and a relationship model that includes a person or team working closely enough with the company to ensure they produce the results they need. However, those benefits come with prices higher than both models to the left on the continuum. The concessions clients make in this model include a lack of strategic outcomes and higher costs than the greater value strategy. Solving the problem with a solution is often enough to win the client's business, but it does little to improve their broader problem-solving outcomes.

One challenge we face as salespeople is that this *solution*-delivery model has been thoroughly and completely commoditized, so a given product or service is not always different enough from a competitor's to create a preference. A similar challenge is presented by all legacy approaches: The approach and solutions are largely indistinguishable. We are commoditized at this level, with clients seeming to prefer the status quo to buying something "new" that is indistinguishable from what they already have.

Strategic Partners

At the far right of the continuum, you find companies that compete by having the highest price but creating the most value for their clients, largely coming from their advice, their recommendations, and their commitment to their clients. While they may occasionally have problems with execution or delivery, they are capable and profitable enough to solve them quickly. This model comes with only one concession: a higher price. That concession is difficult for some clients to make, sometimes because they are trying to be thrifty, and sometimes because their own delivery model doesn't allow for that level of investment. Even a high-value model may prevent you from pursuing companies with a different model.

While I love this model and its ability to generate strategic outcomes, the market is smaller because for a great deal of customers and clients, good enough is good enough. However, when a certain result is critical, this model fares well. Don't worry if this isn't your company's model; all of the models have concessions that make them vulnerable to the others if the context of the decision is wrong. On the left side of the value continuum, the compelling question is "Why would you pay more than necessary?" On the right, it becomes "what happens when you fail your clients or customers?"

Fighting on Two Fronts

The lowest-price model competes primarily with the model to its right (scalable commodity) while the highest-price delivery model mainly competes with its neighbor to the left (solutions), since there's no competition to the right. The two models in the middle, the scalable commodity and the solution, both fight on two fronts, with a threat on each side: One has attractively lower prices and the other creates greater value. It's important to recognize the distinction between price and cost, and it's even more critical that you use the right words to describe the different models. A model with the lowest prices isn't the one with the lowest cost: your client would pay for every concession their supplier requires of them, whether they know it or not. The high-est price almost always creates lower overall costs over time, due to eliminating any concessions.

No matter the delivery model, there is always a way to posi-tion your competitor to the left as being inadequate due to the concessions it demands. You can also attack your competitor to the right by explaining why the greater value they create isn't worth paying extra for when good enough is good enough. Being in one of the two middle delivery models means executing the Goldilocks strategy of being just right, dismissing your adjacent competitors as too hot or too cold.

A Choice of Two Concessions

Your clients are always forced to choose between higher prices and lower value. When they choose a specific model, they take all the problems and challenges they will experience once they work with their new partner or supplier. As we've seen, lower prices don't mean lower costs. But no salesperson would say, "We have the lowest price, but our deliveries will be routinely late, some of what we send you won't be right, and your customers will return more of what you sell them. You are going to spend a lot on rework, and you may need to hire a couple more people in customer service." Conversely, the problem for those who have a high-price model is that there is no way to hide their pricing. For a lot of companies with this model, the higher price they charge is the only real concession they are asking the client to make. They charge more so they have the profit margin to deliver the better results their clients need.

The best time to discuss these concessions is before the client decides. Yet most salespeople provide a proposal and their pricing without ever positioning their offering. This is a great opportu-nity to play our favorite game, "I know something you don't know. May I share it with you?" With a single question in a discovery call, you can create an opening for this conversation: "Have you decided what delivery model will provide the best results for you?" Said another way, "What different approaches are you considering?" By exposing that the client is unaware of the different models in your industry, and eventually by teaching them how those models work, you close the gap and create an information parity that enables your client to choose wisely, because you have exposed them to information unavailable to them.

Buyer's Remorse

By triangulating your competition, you are enabling your client to recognize two things. First, they really can differentiate between their options based on how they work. Second, they can't escape the choices each model imposes on them. When your client mistakenly chooses a model with a low price and undisclosed concessions, their buyer's remorse comes from not understanding the importance of choosing the right delivery model. When your client realizes that they are paying too much and cannot capture the value of a higher price, their remorse comes from a lack of information. Information disparity—not problems with price or quality—is the real source of buyer's remorse.

When you have seller's remorse, there is more than a good chance you sold your client something that was the wrong delivery model for both of you. The limits of your model can cause you to fail your clients. Whenever you experience an unhappy client who wants better results than they will pay for, you have a mismatch of investment and outcomes. When you use the highest-price, greatest-value model, not delivering on your promise results in the same mismatch. While I am wary of qualifying, there is a tremendous value to recognizing that the way you deliver value is a mismatch and bowing out of the competition. It is the easiest of all decisions to walk away from a client with expectations larger than their checkbook.

Teaching the Models and One-Up Positioning

From your newly triangulated position, not only are you One-Up when compared to your client, but you are also One-Up over your competition. Most important, you are an expert in your industry, and an expert in helping your clients improve their results, an outcome you create by helping them understand and carefully consider their decisions. This approach facilitates sense-making, enabling the client to recognize and weight the factors they will need to consider with your help. The central tenet running through this work is that the only real differentiation you can create is the sales conversation. As part of that conversation, a triangulation strategy gives you the ability to differentiate your model from your competition's model. Two companies with similar offerings can produce wildly different results, due to the nature of the value they create, how they deliver it, and how they compete in their space.

To summarize, in a conversation with your client, you can start by explaining that there are several primary delivery models in your industry, each with different advantages and disadvantages. Positioning yourself at the top of the triangle, you sing the praises of each model (advantages) before confessing their sins (concessions), and spelling out the challenges the client will experience from each model. A question that will do you a lot better than "What's keeping you up at night?" is "Have you decided which of the four delivery models makes the most sense for the outcomes you need now?" There is little chance that your client has ever heard this question, so it exposes an area where they are almost certain to be One-Down and allows them to become One-Up, by learning how to understand the value of each model and their limitations (yours included).

Your industry might have more or fewer models. To execute this strategy, use as many models as necessary but as few as possible. Four models work for most industries, providing enough differentiation without having too many similar models. The key to succeeding with this strategy requires that you recognize and understand the different models, so you can explain each one's pros and cons. You will not be considered an honest broker if you are unwilling to include the value of a competing model or the concessions of your own model.

The point of triangulation is not just to prove that your model is the best fit, but to transcend the competition among models. You become far more valuable to your potential client when you can give them an objective assessment of their choices and explain the rules of the game to them, making you not just a player but a commentator and referee rolled into one. A client who is uncertain gains a lot of certainty this way, not just about their decision but about your suitability to help them make sense of their world. The person who provides the client with an education on the different models, their advantages, their challenges, and the concessions they are agreeing to is the person who is best positioned to win the client's business. By being One-Up, you become the third force in the debate.

11

Being One-Up Helps Your Clients Change

Experience is a hard teacher because she gives the test first, the lesson afterwards.

—Vern Law

MY MAIN CONTACT called me while I was in New York City. He was frantic, talking so fast that I could barely understand him at first. It was the middle of his company's peak season, and they had just won four new, very large clients. They were having trouble staffing their business, so the senior leadership team was flying in to deal with the problem. My client said the COO had asked for me to come and meet with their team. I told him to slot me in at 11:00 a.m. so I could take the next flight out from JFK.

The client's problem had started years before this phone call. For four years, I had been warning the local leadership and their senior leaders that the way they were operating would cause them to fail. While I am no Nostradamus, it was easy to deduce that their failure would come in the fourth quarter, a time of year when labor in their industry was scarce. The company repeatedly made two mistakes certain to harm their business. First, they kept their pay rates so low that they fell behind the market. Second, they were terrible to the people we provided them. In one exit interview, an employee described their facility as a cross between a daycare center and a maximum-security prison, a statement not designed to be a compliment. My sister coined the phrase "You can treat people like shit, or you can pay them like shit, but you can't do both." Naturally, my client was guilty on both charges and unwilling to change.

When I showed up to their facility, I was ushered into a conference room where seven senior leaders were discussing their problem, and the blunt, take-no-prisoners chief operating officer was writing on a gigantic whiteboard. I watched him pretend not to see me enter the room, a move designed to create a power dynamic in his favor; I would have to wait for him, despite flying to the meeting at his request. I tried to hide my smile: He had to

193

have someone call me to come and tell him what he needed to do to salvage his quarter and his clients. There was no doubt that he was One-Down: He knew it, I knew it, and everyone in the room knew it. When the COO finished writing down yet another buzzword that would do nothing to help change his company's fortune, he turned to me and immediately went on the attack: "You haven't provided us a single person this week. You are failing us. I want you to tell me what you are going to do about it."

I replied, "There is nothing I can do to help you. In fact, no one can help you now. You are not going to get a single person to take a job here because you pay too little. Your pay rate is twenty-five percent behind the market."

My answer frustrated him enough to try another power play. He stormed over to where I was sitting, got in my face, and shouted, "Just two hours ago, your competitor sat in that same chair and told us that the pay rate is not a problem!"

I calmly countered, "In the past four days, none of the four companies you are working with have been able to provide you a single employee."

Still looming above me, he demanded, "Are you saying he is lying?"

I looked right into his eyes. "No, he's just afraid of you."

There was a pause in the conversation that made everyone in the room uncomfortable, except me and the COO. After a few seconds, though, he broke, at last admitting his One-Down status: "What do we need to spend to get the people we need?" I gave him the precise figure, knowing that his labor expenses would never come close to fitting the budget model on the spreadsheet dominating his decisions.

Neither of us was happy. He did not want to spend the money, and I was disappointed that I could not compel the change the company needed to make before it harmed their business. It wasn't for a lack of trying, but I simply did not execute the certainty sequence correctly: I failed to create the certainty of negative consequences. The reason that companies and their leaders don't change is because they don't recognize how close those negative consequences are. Some go to the doctor, discover that they haven't been taking care of themselves, and commit to a diet and exercise regimen that starts improving their health. Others hear the same advice and do nothing until they have a heart attack, at which point they finally believe the doctor's orders. Some of your clients and prospects will heed your warnings and follow your advice. Others, however, will need to fail before they change.

If you were hoping for a happy ending to this story, I am afraid I can only disappoint you. Over the few next weeks, my client did manage to hire more than enough employees, but demand was so high that they didn't have time to train them—and one by one, they lost three of their four new accounts. Two weeks later, my six-million-dollar nightmare of a client fired me and my company. It was a tough loss, but I live by Bloom's commandment: "Tell the truth at any price, even the price of your deal." Being One-Up means you can't be bought.

This story is one of a small handful where the truth came at a high price. Fortunately, these events are eclipsed by the many clients who changed before they were harmed. They took the advice and recommendations I offered them and improved their results. The reason I push my clients to change on their own timeline is because when they don't, the outcome is often dictated by forces they can't control. You must likewise help your client change when they need to, even if they resist any change at all, because postponing the change may make it impossible.

How to Be Truly Consultative

There are a lot of ideas about what makes up a consultative approach. I would argue that it is not simply asking good questions, even though they are necessary to properly diagnose the client's need and recognize what they need to do to improve things. Part of being consultative is leveraging business acumen, situational knowledge (experience), and a recognition of what your client needs to do. Consultation also does not mean avoiding high-pressure tactics, because the absence of an old-school approach is not evidence of a consultative approach. By definition, the word "consultative" means to provide professional advice and recommendations. That's a good start, but let me offer you another test to determine whether your approach is truly consultative: "Did your client change?"

Even when I was succeeding in sales, I was not consultative until my clients took my advice outside of hiring me and my company. As you have discovered, the fact that you displaced your competition and helped them carry their old solution out the door does not mean you are consultative. The same advice my nightmare client rejected for years resonated with other clients, especially when they changed before they lost the chance to do so on their own terms.

Most One-Down salespeople believe that their "solution" is the largest part of the value they create for their clients. Being One-Up means believing and behaving as if the solution is only a relatively small part of the value you create. In some cases, your "solution" is actually the least valuable part of your consultation, with the sales conversation making up a much greater part of the value.

Turn and Face the Strange

Some of the largest changes you can help your clients make lie outside of your solution. These changes often contribute more to the client's better results than any other factor, yet many salespeople still believe that offering genuinely valuable advice is outside their sales role. Here is the One-Up paradox: Your clients often believe that they can improve their results by changing their supplier and their solution, ignoring their part in their poor performance. If you enable or even share that belief, then your client will replace you when you fail because of something your client refuses to change. If you haven't already had this experience in your sales career, it's only a matter of time.

Every client you work with is doing something to sabotage their own better outcomes, either by choosing the wrong actions or refusing to choose the right ones. For the client to improve their results, they have to change. That can make for an intimidating conversation, but being One-Up means fearing the right danger. A One-Down salesperson fears making the client angry by addressing their client's role in their poor results, when what they should fear is allowing their client to fail. Being One-Up means helping your clients recognize everything they need to change to improve their results—not just their supplier and their solution. A good advisor tells you the truth about what you need to do. A weak one allows you to continue to do something that harms you, a One-Down position that elevates being pliable and liked over being respected and trusted. Because you are dead set on helping your clients improve their results, you must have those difficult conversations, even the ones that require a great deal of diplomacy and good timing.

In a previous book, I wrote, "Selling isn't something you do to someone. It's something you do for and with someone, and for their benefit." It's easier to make a difference for others when you occupy the One-Up position, a space that allows you to use your expertise to help others solve their problems, address their challenges, and improve their results—and perhaps even their lives. This makes being One-Up irresistible for those who want to make real change and make a difference. Remember, you find your clients with uncertainty, so you compel change by providing the certainty of negative consequences. Once they are compelled, they face the uncertainty of change. You compel them to act by providing them the certainty they can and will succeed to change and produce the better outcomes you can help them achieve.

Addressing Larger Organizational Concerns

The reason clients with real problems and challenges refuse to change is because they believe that the risk of change is greater than the damage from their current problems. Knowing that larger organizational challenges prevent your clients from changing allows you to address their real concerns, not just their superficial objections, and improves your results. A client has no reason to buy from someone who can't read between the lines or is afraid to address the concerns that prevent change. Yet many salespeople fear that even bringing up these concerns might frighten away a client—let alone proactively addressing them. When a One-Down salesperson hears the words "now is not a good time," they often misinterpret it. That statement isn't an objection; it's the masked expression of a concern, one you must resolve for and with your client to allow them to move forward. Here are the key organizational concerns you must resolve.

- **What If It Doesn't Work?** When compelling a significant change, you are asking your client to step into the unknown with you. Even though the One-Up approach has gotten you this far, you can still expect your client to be concerned about failing. The One-Down decision to avoid this conversation may cause your client to become more concerned the closer they get to a decision. The One-Up alternative is to instigate a conversation about how you will ensure your client succeeds. Doing so earlier in the sales conversation will provide you with the time you need to have the conversations, provide proof, and create the certainty for you to move forward together.
- **What If It Makes Things Worse?** The only thing worse than a malfunctioning solution is one that actually makes things worse. Any client who has ever changed, only to be

confronted by even more difficult problems and challenges, may well be once bitten, twice shy when it comes to the change you propose. Addressing this concern requires you to explain the steps and stages necessary to produce the better results, perhaps coupled with how you will mitigate common problems your client might have on their way to better results.

- **What If You Don't Support Us?** Your client does not yet know where you will be if the train runs off the track. Will you be standing next to them, helping them to make the change you recommended, or will you disappear without a trace? You create certainty when you explain how you will support your client's transformation.

- **What If People Resist?** When people who are not part of the decision will be, willingly or unwillingly, part of the potential change, a client will have every reason to worry that some of them will resist that change. The vantage point insight that consensus is necessary to change initiatives allows you to get in front of this potential showstopper. In a consensus sale, you might help create certainty by saying, "We should have one more meeting with our team and your leaders to make sure we are all prepared to deal with any challenges that might cause your team to be concerned. They need to know we're all here to help." By committing your team to be there if there are problems, you make it easier for your client's team to commit to their part of the work.

You may address the first three concerns as you work toward the commitment to decide: "Let me share our implementation and execution plan to show you how we are going to make this change, and what contingency plans we have in place should we have any problems. This is the team that is going to be on point, working closely with you."

Individual Concerns

There are a couple of potential concerns that can cause individual decision-makers to avoid change. You will need to address these carefully, generally in conversations with only a few people in the room.

Position   An individual concerned about losing their position or status won't often tell you directly that any serious challenge, problem, or failure will come at a price that it is too high for them. I cringe when I hear salespeople tell a prospective client they will be a "hero" or a "rock star," a gambit designed to appeal to egomaniacs. Besides being disingenuous, this gambit can backfire by making the contact worry about their position should things go badly. As the person who is One-Up, you are better off explaining what you and your company will do to ensure your client succeeds, including your contingency plans for the inevitable issues that come with any change.

Responsibility or Blame   Any stakeholder pursuing an important or necessary change may fear being blamed for its failure or any challenges that come with that change. Some people have a hidden commitment to avoiding trouble, blame, or responsibility when things go wrong. Some people's fear of being blamed exceeds their hope of being thought of as a good leader or decision-maker. Unaddressed concerns can cause your client to disengage, stalling or ending any opportunity for better results. Treating any concern as if it is unwarranted may likewise cause a contact to oppose an initiative, even if it is critical to their success.

One of the reasons clients worry about being blamed is because previous One-Down salespeople and sales organizations avoided the client when they had problems executing a solution. You can call this "the foxhole problem"—when your contact is in the middle of a challenge, they need you or someone from your company standing in the foxhole with them, not abandoning them to deal with the problem alone. You have to create the certainty that you and your team will be there. You can say, "We are not going to let you struggle or fail here. We have the support of our entire executive team to provide whatever resources you need to get this done." For you to say this, though, it has to be true: being One-Up means selling inside your organization, too.

As you get closer to a decision, you'll find an increase in concerns. The more significant the change, the greater the concern. The last part of the certainty sequence requires that you create enough certainty of positive outcomes to overcome the natural resistance to change, which is driven by fear and doubt. While most of this book has been about compelling change, helping your contacts make good decisions, advising them, and leading your clients to better results, addressing concerns is a good way to create certainty of positive results.

Viewing the sales conversation through the lens of certainty can enhance the intentions and behaviors that soothe uncertainty and help contacts move forward to better results. The point is not to remove the risk completely, but to make it easier for your clients to move forward in spite of the risk. Helping your clients gain the certainty to change, confidence in their initiative and their partner, and assurance they can and will succeed enables them to move forward with their decision and your deal.

How to Present and Propose Your Initiative

Your legacy approach might require you to answer the "why us" question during your first meeting, a conversation out of sync with the client's primary concern: whether you are worth their time. What follows is a structure that will allow you to present and propose your initiative so it allows you to address "why us" in a meaningful way, after you have proved it through the sales conversation. (If you haven't already proven you are the right choice by this point, nothing you say will change any minds.)

- **The Current State.** The best place to start a presentation is the client's current state, one in which they are facing current or imminent poor results. Here you are reminding your client about why they need to change, allowing you to point to the forces driving their challenges. Chances are, you'll have to take the first eight or twelve "why us" slides and move them to the back of your slide deck, where they belong. You are also going to need a new set of slides that answer the question "Why change?"
- **The Future State.** You follow the current state by describing the better, future state your client company needs to create with and through your help and guidance. Use present tense here to associate your proposal with reaching that future state (e.g., "XYZ Widgets has a daily throughput of 1,200 widgets"). Emphasize the primary future outcomes you and your client will create while working together.
- **Your Initiative.** In this section of your presentation and proposal, you want to describe exactly what both you and your client will do to bring that future state to life. Depending on the complexity of what you sell and what you and your contacts need to do, you may need a project plan, a timeline, milestones, or some other way of describing what each party will need to do.

   Producing better results will partly come from whatever you sell, but also from the changes your client will need to make. Until now, it is unlikely that anyone has told you directly that your client has to have skin in the game, committing to make the changes that will allow them to co-create the future state. In my experience, at least, when your contacts don't do their part, they're likely to blame you for their poor results or failures.

■ **Why Us.** Having already proven "why us," now you can address it, but not in the way you might think. Instead of creating credibility, you are focused on creating certainty, the natural next step in the progression. When you speak about your company, instead of talking about how long you have been in business, talk about how you have gained the experience to create the better results your client needs. Instead of talking about your senior leadership team, talk about the resources to be assigned or available to ensure your contacts succeed. When you point to whatever you sell, explain how that will contribute to the better results—when combined with the changes the client must make for this to work.

Responding to Stakeholder Questions

Even if they don't say them out loud, the stakeholders you're working with will have questions about your presentation proposal. Design your presentation and proposal to address each of the questions below.

Is This the Right Decision? It is easy to decide when a purchase is nothing more than a transaction. When there are no real or lasting negative consequences for making a poor decision, investing a little money and time is no big deal. If what you buy doesn't work, you replace it. However, when the decision is one your client is rarely charged to make, and when failure comes with potentially devastating negative consequences, the increased risk often looms larger than the problem your client is trying to solve. This is the nature of complex sales, the decisions that require the assistance of a One-Up, truly consultative salesperson.

When a result is critical to your client's business, the people making that decision will naturally have concerns about change. No one wants to decide to change, only to find themselves unprepared for a new and different set of challenges. The responsibility to change also comes with accountability for the results, whether good or awful. One reason clients don't change, even when it is necessary, is because they lack the certainty that they are making the right decision.

You want to address this question in the "Current State" and "Future State" sections, reminding your audience why they need change and why this is the right decision now.

Is This the Right Answer?   The client who's trying to determine whether they should change now or continue to muddle through is also trying to gain enough confidence to do something new and different. The reason they keep asking you, "Will this work?" is because they're asking each other the same question. A lack of certainty in a potential initiative can make it difficult for your contacts to change.

Greater certainty that the solution will work increases the client's certainty about both the deal and the broader change. One way you create certainty in the solution is by building consensus with the people deciding—as well as the people who will need to execute your solution. Speeding through or bypassing the conversations that create certainty will tip the balance for inaction. The more certainty your contacts have around your answer to their challenges, the easier it is to select you and to brave the risks of changing how they do business.

You address this in the section where you provide the initiative, proving it's the right answer by tying it back to the outcomes.

Can We Execute and Succeed?   One of the internal conversations your clients are engaged in is whether they can execute your solution and make the change they are pursuing. The fear of failure is a powerful force when it comes to change. Any concerns about an inability to produce better results can make it easier for the client to do nothing. One mistake that causes uncertainty is not explaining exactly what changes your client will need to make—all the things they will need to do to produce the results they need.

Failing to provide a realistic plan or downplaying the challenges may seem reassuring, but it can actually create greater uncertainty. Even though you might fear describing the work the client must do and the challenges you must overcome together, that conversation demonstrates that you are aware of your client's risk, that you have analyzed and have experience dealing with those challenges, and that you know how to dispatch any problems that would prevent success.

The "Your Initiative" section needs to provide the certainty that your client can execute and succeed. Sometimes, you need greater detail here to create certainty and the confidence to move forward.

Are You the Right Partner?   Your prospective client is also trying to gain certainty about who will provide the solution. When contacts cannot confidently select a partner, the need to change and the right solution may not be enough to let the client change. You must primarily answer this question through the sales conversation, but you can reinforce it through the first three sections of your proposal and presentation, pointing to the current state, the future state, and the initiative that will deliver the results.

If you have done the work recommended in this book, you will find it easy to prove that you are the right partner to guide your client to better results. If you haven't, nothing you can say about your experience or your client list will make a difference.

12

Advice for Those Who Are Presently One-Down

The true value of sword-fencing cannot be seen within the confines of sword-fencing technique.
—Miyamoto Musashi, The Book of Five Rings

BEING ONE-UP MAY sound intimidating, but remember that anyone who is now One-Up started One-Down. There are no shortcuts to being One-Up: You can't buy a stairway, you can't fake it, and you certainly can't cheat your way in. Like success itself, it requires that you do the work. The level of competency needed to become and stay One-Up means you must do the work to make most of your competition One-Down and no threat to you in a contest for your dream client's business. How could occupying that space not be worth every second of work?

A person who is One-Down will stay One-Down until they take the actions necessary to become One-Up. Fortunately, the time and effort you invest in developing yourself and your approach is largely within your control. If you're ready to acquire the knowledge, experience, and understanding that will let you offer your counsel, your advice, and your recommendations, this chapter (along with the accompanying *One-Up Workbook* - www.theoneupsale.com) will help you get started.

The Starting Line: Intentionally Intentional

Here at the start of your journey to One-Upness, you need to recognize a key truth about being One-Up that will motivate you to move confidently toward your goal: the large majority of salespeople are not One-Up, regardless of how many years they have worked in sales. In fact, many of the salespeople who brag about how long they've worked don't realize that they've essentially repeated the same year over and over.

While experience is important, only thoughtful people who are willing to process their learning and activate those lessons in the field can be One-Up. This explains why some spend their whole careers One-Down while a relative newcomer can occupy the One-Up

209

space. The difference is intentionality: you must actively leverage every insight, every experience, and every interaction into becoming One-Up. Everything can and should teach you how to sell better, even (especially) the mistakes you make along the way.

If you want to be One-Up, you have to be intentional in several areas. Without the intention to become One-Up, you will fail to process the experiences that might contribute to your development in a way that improves your abilities. As you do your work, you must commit to active learning: analyzing and operationalizing everything you do to make your next day (week, month, quarter, etc.) better.

Every interaction with a client, pursuit of a deal, opportunity capture, or lost deal brings with it a lesson—or multiple lessons. What will make you One-Up is deriving and processing those lessons. You will be tempted to go through the motions instead of writing down your experience and processing it to see what you learned. (I only know what I know because I write everything down, normally resulting in a thousand-word blog post every twenty-four hours.) And don't just write down results; pay attention to everything you see, hear, feel, and experience as you sell. Only by intentionally doing this work will you be able to see something others can never see.

The One-Up Mindset

Before we get practical and tactical, you need to have the appropriate mindset. You may find some elements of this mindset to be uncomfortable at first, but later they'll provide you with a competitive advantage. These mindsets are like a turbo boost for your development, letting you speed by others who will seem to be sitting still.

You Are Responsible for Your Own Development

One-Down salespeople often avoid taking responsibility, the subject of the first two components of the One-Up mindset. The first area where you need to take full and complete control over your burgeoning capacity to be One-Up is your personal and professional development. You are the greatest asset you will ever have for producing the results you want throughout your life. You are, however, a bit of a fixer-upper. You could use a little work, or maybe more than a little.

People generally invest in people who invest in themselves. However, you cannot wait for your company, your manager, or anyone else to invest in your development. That's been my own pattern for many years, even outside the office. When I was a kid playing rock 'n' roll, I was trained by a voice teacher, something I paid for myself even when I had too little money. I started college when I was twenty-six years old, going to classes from 6:00 p.m. to 9:00 p.m., three nights a week, so I could work full time. I attended law school after college, keeping that same schedule (though adding a few kids) for three more years. Even today, I put a lot of time and resources into a whole range of personal or professional development programs.

One reason I keep learning is that my disciplines and insights bleed into other areas of my life. I am confident that whether you study chess, take a hip-hop dance class, or discover how to paint with watercolors, you will learn not only the curriculum but also a great deal about yourself.

Everything Is My Fault

One of the most debilitating mindsets a person can have is the belief that external factors are responsible for their results or their circumstances. When you ask your ego to find a reason for your failure or your challenging circumstances, it will offer you a dozen ways to absolve you of responsibility. Believing what that ego tells you will not only skew your vision of reality, but will also stunt your growth by preventing you from learning something from your experiences—especially the negative experiences that teach you how to avoid repeating the same mistakes.

If you believe that you only lost a big deal because your competitor offered the client a lower price, that belief will stop you from recognizing that you need to work on your triangulation strategy. How did you allow your client to believe "good enough" is good enough? Recognizing that you did not do enough to help the client understand the difference in your delivery models and the concessions your competitor requires gives you the possibility (and hopefully the motivation) to do something different. When your low-priced competitor fails the client, you have a data point that allows you to better describe the perils of believing that a lower price means a lower cost in your industry.

Seeking excuses leaves you One-Down far longer than necessary. Taking absolute responsibility for every part of your life and your results will find you racing toward being One-Up. If everything is your fault, you are empowered to do something about it, but only if you discover the lesson.

Curiosity Does Not Kill Cats

Whenever you see an old cat, it's probably on life eight or nine. My youngest daughter has a scalawag of a cat who lost one of its nine lives by walking a bit too carelessly along the upstairs banister in our home. My whole family heard him hit the floor of the foyer with a thud. The cat was fine, but he did not repeat his mistake. His next life included the experience that took his previous one, making him a bit bruised but slightly more One-Up.

You might be curious by disposition. Some of us are insatiably driven to understand our world. I spent my teenage years trying desperately to drop out of high school. I loved learning, but there was not much of an opportunity to achieve that at my second high school. My first high school would have been more conducive to learning, but I was ungovernable at thirteen. I spent little time at either school, but I read books and got a certain type of education that one can only acquire on the street. It doesn't matter if the Ivy League (or any college) never came calling, though, because another education is available.

Becoming One-Up means exercising your curiosity to understand. Anyone trying to help another person make better decisions and improve their results damn well better have a good understanding of what they are teaching. Curiosity is the desire to understand. You cannot be a sense maker without being curious (and industrious) enough to learn thoroughly enough that you can impart your understanding to your client.

Seek Mastery of Your Craft

One difference between a person who is One-Up and one who is One-Down is their commitment to mastery. A person who is One-Down may well go "all in" on learning a new skill—buying all the books, taking the classes, securing professional gear, and doing everything in their power to look the part. But they never open the books, let alone act on what they learned. They may attend the class, but they never do the work necessary to improve. Their mastery stops and ends with illusion.

Those who seek One-Up mastery of any art, craft, or profession do the work without fail. They don't just read the books and take the courses, but also put in the work to change their strategies, tactics, beliefs, and behaviors. As George Leonard wrote in the wonderful little book *Mastery*, those who master anything stay on the mat longer than anyone else. They live through the plateaus, the time where they are doing the work without getting any better. Eventually, they experience a breakthrough and level up.

Leonard described One-Down learners as "dabblers," but I prefer to call them "poseurs," a term from my time playing rock 'n' roll. I can't count how many guys would grow their hair long, pick up an *ax* (never calling it a mere *guitar*), and try desperately to look like they were in a band, when they couldn't even play a chord. Don't dabble: Whatever you do, if you want to be One-Up, seek mastery.

Impatient Patience

Mastery takes time. You want to be impatient to act but patient as it pertains to your results. Reversing that order creates problems around mastery. Waiting around to act will slow your development, taking more time than necessary to acquire the experience you need to improve your results. Being impatient about your results may cause you to give up before you have done enough work, over time, to reach a certain milestone. Here's the thing: It is very difficult for you to measure the small, incremental gains you make from day to day or week to week. With client conversations, for instance, you can improve without even recognizing that you have improved. But improving by 1 percent per day for a whole year adds up to an increase of almost 38 percent.

I used to practice aikido, a Japanese martial art that is rather difficult and technical. After a year, I was frustrated at my lack of progress, even though I practiced with only the best martial artists. I couldn't see my own development until a new class started and I realized how much better I was than the brand-new students. My mistake was comparing myself to the One-Up teachers who had trained me, rather than the One-Down students I was actually competing against. Just do the work and don't worry too much about anything else. You will make progress.

Organizing Your Insights

Every experience brings the opportunity to discover something about yourself, your world, your clients, their world, and/or how to improve your clients' experience in the sales conversation. There are always new lessons and learning for those who seek them. But the insights you gain through your experience are only available if you do the work of processing and organizing your learning.

The rest of this chapter will provide you with the strategies and tactics that will speed your development and move you swiftly toward being One-Up. The practices here will serve you well throughout your career in sales, and in every other area of your life. Being One-Up is a project with a beginning, but no end.

Read Widely and Consistently

You can become One-Up simply by allowing your interests to drive you to learn more and understand better. Reading is the most consistent way to gain One-Up advantages. For $27, six hours of your time, and a willingness to act on what you learned, you get the same knowledge as a person who spent the largest part of their life learning. You literally pay that person (or at least their publisher) a fraction of a penny for every hour they spent learning, practicing, and organizing their knowledge and insight.

Here are two reading habits that will speed you on your way to being One-Up. First, read for the last hour you are awake. Pick up a hardcover book and a pencil, then mark the things you read that capture your attention. Second, sometime the next day, review and rewrite those passages in your own words. The consistency of reading and writing down what you believe is useful will speed up your journey.

Classic literature will teach much about the one thing you need to understand more than anything else: human beings. But read whatever interests you and feeds your curiosity.

Act Like an Apprentice

A few hundred years ago, most families sent their teenagers away to become apprentices. Being an apprentice was not a pleasant experience. You were basically working for free, subject to the whims of your master, to acquire a skill that would eventually allow you to provide for yourself and your family. We call this true competency transfer. While I am not suggesting that you move in with the local blacksmith and work for free, I am suggesting that you act like an apprentice.

Because you are trying to acquire a complex set of competencies that make you One-Up, working alongside others who are already One-Up will provide you with examples you can mimic, model, and master. Asking coworkers to let you join their sales calls may seem like bothering them, but it's actually a smart approach to improving your abilities. One thing you might do to pay your keep is to be their sales call scribe, taking notes for them and summarizing all the questions they asked and their contacts' answers. There is a bit of selfish motive here since those notes will also accelerate your development. Asking a One-Up salesperson to explain why they asked the questions they asked or answered the client's questions a certain way will teach you how they think and why they do things the way they do.

Enroll in a Martial Art

You will find that being in sales comes with conflict, but (generally) not the kind that requires you to defend yourself from violence. Studying martial arts causes you to experience a controlled type of physical violence. You'll also learn two important skills.

First, you will learn to be more disciplined, something that is difficult to obtain but makes everything else easier. Second, you will learn not to fear conflict. It's important that you respect your client, but you should never be afraid of them or of causing conflict. You will have to say no to your clients, and you will have to give them bad news. You want to enter into any necessary conflict from the position of One-Up.

Journal Your Experiences

One of the best ways to teach yourself to be One-Up is to document your experiences. There is something powerful in human development that is found in writing down your experiences. A friend of mine is a Zen master. At dinner one evening, he told me about one great Zen master who never meditated, finding the same benefit from writing down his thoughts and processing his experiences. Writing allows you to look at your subjective experiences objectively.

There are excellent note-taking apps out there, so you can organize your experiences and what they have taught you about yourself, your clients, or your world. As you add experiences and review past experiences, you see things you could not perceive until you acquired more experience. In twenty minutes a day, you can make better sense of your experiences and how to use them to better help your clients out of their One-Down position.

Start a Decision Journal

This practice isn't easy to keep up, but I've found it very beneficial to being One-Up, especially in terms of gaining confidence in my advice and my recommendations. Here's how a decision journal works. Whenever you have a significant decision to make, write down your choice and explain why you believe it to be the right decision. Later, record the outcome of the decision, right or wrong.

Over time, you'll recognize the second-order effects: not just the direct consequences of the action but also the subsequent consequences that followed. As you make more decisions to create and win new clients and new opportunities, your thinking will improve, even if mostly through making poor decisions. You can keep these notes in your existing journal, along with the next journal you should keep.

Prediction Journal

Another way to improve your One-Upness is to write down what you believe will happen in a given arena and why. As you acquire knowledge, experience, and insights, making predictions about what you believe will happen helps you think better by measuring your results. I am good at making predictions about the future because I make them infrequently and only in areas where I am One-Up, learning from others' predictions where I am One-Down.

If my experience is a guide, you can expect your predictions to be wrong when you were missing information, misinterpreted information, or were way too aggressive or optimistic, causing you to miss your timeline. My best strategy to predict the future is to look back at how humans have acted in the past.

Gaining Field Expertise

You need to become an expert in your field to be truly consultative and One-Up. Some of the expertise will take time, but you can accelerate your timeline by working harder to learn what you need to know. I can still tell you all the main statistics of the current labor market, a habit I picked up by reading and listening to them each week. I can also hit you with a bunch of stats and citations about the world of B2B sales.

I think of these stats as hooks on a wall, the kind where you might hang your coat or your car keys when you get home. As the statistics change, I swap out the old data for the new, a practice that works well for keeping up to speed on what's going on in my world. While it's impressive to walk your client through a slide deck with your insights and supporting data, it's even more powerful when you can do it from memory, something that looks like magic, especially when you can weave your insights and supporting data into any conversation.

We're more than halfway through. Let me warn you now that the next three practices are much more difficult—and much more powerful—than anything most salespeople will even try. However, there is no reason for you to stop here when you are capable of so much more.

Ask Your Clients to Teach You

A person who is One-Down will avoid asking their client questions about their business or industry (no, "What's keeping you up at night?" doesn't count), fearing their client will think less of them for not knowing something. There is no shame in being ignorant, a word that simply means you lack specific knowledge or awareness, but giving into that fear prolongs your ignorance far longer than necessary. Anyone who possesses the knowledge or awareness you lack was every bit as ignorant as you are before they were educated—or more likely, before someone else educated them. Asking someone else to help you understand allows them to move you away from One-Down and toward One-Up.

In a recent negotiation with a client, for example, I ran into a contractual issue, one that would have ended our potential deal. As I explained my side of the conflict, I went over what I would do and what I could not do. The counsel for my client said, "We have language that we use in situations like this. I'll send it to you." I had no idea this language existed or that it was widely used to get to a deal. Since then, I've used that language to negotiate eight other contracts.

Earlier in this book, you learned that you and your client are both One-Up and One-Down. Where you are One-Up and your client is One-Down, what you know improves their position. But the opposite is also true. When your client is One-Up and you are One-Down, what they know will give you the chance to become One-Up. I will also remind you that you should not be a know-it-all, but you cannot be a know-nothing. You are best served by being a "knows-quite-a-lot about something." No one, including you, should expect you to know everything.

Acquiring Lenses and Sense-Making

There are people whose view of the world isn't one you have ever seen. They write books, they record podcasts, they run YouTube channels, and they share their views with others to help them make sense of the world. You have to acquire a set of lenses that allows you to make sense of your own world before you can do the same for your clients. Without giving you a list of specific people to follow, let me point you in a particular direction.

You are looking for people with deep insights and the ability to explain some part of your world to you, increasing your ability to see something that others don't see—often because they don't know the view exists. Most people are not curious enough to want to learn to understand their world, let alone teach others to make sense of it. One way you will improve your ability to see through different lenses is to reject the assumption that people with different perspectives are intrinsically different from you.

Start Teaching Others

A certain kind of person bothers other people by sharing with them the things they find interesting and exciting. You have run headlong into at least one of these people, probably while they were standing behind a desk. One way to improve your ability to be One-Up is to teach others, an age-old way to learn something.

Teaching others requires that you understand your subject well enough to transfer that knowledge to others. While that's a good starting point, what's even better and more relevant to being One-Up is taking every opportunity to rehearse. Practicing your lines provides you with confidence, something that will improve your performance when you are face to face with your clients.

A One-Up Curriculum

To develop yourself personally and professionally, start by picking up *The Only Sales Guide You'll Ever Need*. This book will provide you with a competency model that includes the character traits you need to succeed in sales, along with a list of skills required of B2B sales.

The best place for you develop your One-Upness is in the sales conversation. You can speed your development here by listening to and watching salespeople who are already One-Up. You can acquire their language and approach by paying attention to the questions they ask and the language they use to navigate client conversations. Here you should act like an apprentice.

After spending time with One-Up salespeople, the next area you'll want to improve is your vantage point, allowing you to be agile (able to adjust quickly) in facilitating your prospective client's buyer's journey. *The Lost Art of Closing: Winning the 10 Commitments That Drive Sales* provides a road map that will start you down that path if you need help. This is also the first area where you can offer your counsel, your advice, and your recommendations. You want to develop those skills and effective language to guide your clients. Spend time here working on understanding what commitments and conversations benefit your clients, as well as the advice they will need from you.

Once you have an idea about how the sales conversations go in your sales scenarios, you're going to want to start building your One-Upness by identifying the insights that will help you move your clients out of their One-Down position by helping them better understand their world and their decisions about the future. You can treat this as a research project, starting by interviewing One-Up salespeople to help you identify the false assumptions your clients make and the mistakes that follow. You might need to reveal these in the opposite order, asking first for the mistakes and then seeing if you can reverse-engineer the assumptions. You are certain to end up with a list that includes specific behaviors like "buying from a competitor with a lower price," something that isn't as helpful as broader assumptions like "believing that the way they do things now is good enough."

You'll want to go back over Chapter 3 to recognize some of the things that your client doesn't know. Acquire insights that serve your clients by addressing the things they need to know that cannot be easily obtained by a web search—or by asking a One-Down competitor.

The next best place to spend your time and energy is improving your overall approach through a triangulation strategy, so you can provide your client with an understanding of the choices they are going to make and the implications of those decisions. This not only gives your client One-Up insights that can improve their results, but it also positions you to win their business.

At this point in your development, you are prepared to help your clients discover something about themselves. This is impossible if you don't have that lens yourself. So, the order is:

1. See the sales conversation.
2. Recognize the path of conversations and commitments.
3. Develop your insights and recognize areas of disparity.
4. Understand how to teach your clients the different models.
5. Help your clients learn something about themselves.

From this point, you can begin the work of proactively compelling your client to change, something that differentiates the One-Up approach from the legacy approaches. Those older, dated approaches all suggest that your client needs to be "dissatisfied" before you call on them. This is one reason you don't find a "qualifying" stage here, because it suggests that you can't create opportunities that would prevent them from having the problems that legacy approaches allow.

Finally, we come to sense-making and giving a higher-resolution lens, something that will take you more work and time than you like. It will also take both more time and more work than the other strategies. The ability to identify and acquire the lenses that would help you make sense of your world is a critical skill, but one you have to earn by doing the work, including recognizing perspectives with which you may disagree. One-Up awaits.

Warning: The following chapter
contains extreme One-Up tactics that
may not be suitable for all audiences.

13

The Secret Chapter

For what shall it profit a man, if he shall gain the whole world, and lose his own soul?

—Mark 16:26

SOMETIMES, A SOFTER, gentler approach isn't capable of producing One-Up results. When that happens, special tactics are required. These techniques can work for some salespeople in some scenarios, but there is no guarantee any of them will work for you—or that you can even pull them off without blasting your deal to smithereens.

To be clear, the basic One-Up mindset ("I know something you don't know. May I share it with you?") has not changed, nor has the ethical standard laid out at the very beginning of this book. Occasionally, however, it is necessary to directly show your prospective client that they are One-Down. There are times when you will have to point directly at your contact's lack of knowledge, experience, and understanding, none of which judges their intelligence or business acumen. In fact, being smart can cause people to develop blind spots. It can also cause them to believe they know better simply because they have a wall of diplomas and a few sets of letters after their name.

Let me give you an example. A company I invested in was bringing to market a product that created a novel use for nanoparticles. At this time, no one believed it possible to fill a plastic substrate with nanoparticles and run an electric current through it. However, the two founders had discovered a way to do just that. They conferred with scientists, who all insisted their methods were impossible. Those scientists' existing knowledge prevented them from being interested in a new application.

When the founders showed up at the offices of potential clients, they carried in a small plastic block, two wires, and a 12-volt battery. They started by asking the lead scientist to place their hand on the plastic block, explaining that they could remove their hand whenever they decided it was necessary. The plastic heated up extremely fast; within fifteen seconds of the wires being connected to the battery, every scientist who played this game removed their hand. With a tiny amount of current, the inventors explained, you could remove the ice from airplane wings or wind turbines. In the latter case, it could prevent wind farms from shutting down due to ice buildup, which happens over 30 percent of the time.

Even though none of the scientists were burned during the demonstration, it is sometimes necessary for clients to (figuratively) feel some heat before they recognize danger. Sometimes we are so anchored to what we believe that it prevents us from acquiring new insights, new information, and new potential. It's better to avoid things that may harm you without having to suffer from your inability to take in new information.

I advocate for a slightly more direct approach, which is sometimes necessary to keep your contacts away from harm.

How to Position Yourself

In the sales conversation, it's important that you position yourself both as a peer and as the best person to make the decision for the client. If that idea gives you pause, it's because you haven't yet recognized that when you provide your client with your counsel, your advice, and your recommendations, your client ends up making a decision that, largely, you made for them.

You want to show up in your contact's office One-Up, presenting yourself as a person with the knowledge and experience that your contact or stakeholders are lacking. One of the best and most powerful ways to do this without inviting resistance is to start with an executive briefing, something that will allow you to occupy the One-Up position without saying a word about your own degrees or qualifications. Instead, you prove that you have knowledge and experience—with what you sell—that is greater than that of your contacts.

When you begin the sales conversation with a set of insights that explain your client's world, you prove that you have a better and more complete view than they do. You should be able to rattle off all the insights and the data without a slide deck, but use a slide deck anyway to document the data and citations you include. This proves that you have done your homework, something your contact has not done. You also make it easier for your prospective client to believe you when you show them data and the sources. Your One-Up position is supported by experts and their published data and opinions.

This approach has several benefits that the outdated approaches don't provide. First, when you teach, your contact is learning from you. This is as it should be, because you are the expert in producing the better results your prospective client needs. Second, when you have a clearer and more complete view of your client's world than they do, you look, sound, and feel like someone who has done more work than your contacts have done.

Compared to both your contact and any of your competitors, you will appear to be an expert.

One principle I practice is that if something will cause problems later, it's best to prevent it early. You don't want to wait to establish that you are One-Up, and at the same time you want to prevent your clients from believing they are One-Up. That way, they have to wait until you transfer your knowledge and experience to them, helping them become One-Up when compared to their peers and your competition.

How to Engage in Narrative Warfare

Ideas fight for dominance. Because sales is often competitive, you are engaged in a form of narrative warfare. We see this all the time in partisan politics. Every day, Fox News and MSNBC engage in a form of warfare, each trying to create a narrative about how the world works that will win out. Never mind that their audiences are so insular and homogeneous that they change no minds—they will still insist that their view is the only reality.

Triangulation strategy (Chapter 10) is designed to help your contacts to better understand the decision they are making. But there is more to this strategy than meets the eye. While you are providing an education about different business models, you are also burying landmines that prevent your competition from winning otherwise competitive deals. The statements you make as you do this work can provide a narrative that will defeat your competitor's narrative.

After I worked with a client for several years, their corporate office pursued a national contract. Not wanting to lose the only location my company could serve, I engaged in their RFP process. Honoring the truth at any price, I answered the questions honestly, willing to tell the truth and lose rather than lie and win (an approach that allows me to sleep at night). I was the last person to present, something I always request because I want to have the final word. I drove to Chicago by myself, and I walked into the meeting alone. Eleven members of my client's team were sitting around a giant table.

The first person to speak started the conversation by demanding that I explain why I was the only person not to agree to the terms in their RFP. I answered that their pay rate was below market, there was no way to prevent people from missing work, and no one could fill their orders and hours' notice requirements. She then said all of my competitors had agreed to all of their terms and that they wouldn't just lie.

I calmly handed each stakeholder a report with our actual performance analysis, then explained why they had "no shows" and how much time we would need to acquire the employees they needed. When I finished, the company lawyer pointed at me and said, "This is the first honest person to sit in that chair." I won the contract, and a couple days later the head of human resources asked me to choose the staffing company they would use in the states where we did not have offices.

Providing your clients with an education about how your industry works and how to evaluate their decision gives you a chance to inoculate them against being infected with other narratives. After this event, for instance, I told my client, "Anyone who says you won't have people miss work is lying." Several competitors stepped on that landmine.

How to Expose Your Client's Lack of Knowledge and Experience

The best way to expose a client's lack of knowledge and experience is by asking questions you are certain they cannot answer. This directly highlights their One-Down status, so you want to ask the right questions without causing offense or creating any resistance to the knowledge or experience you are trying to impart to them. You can also ask questions you are certain will provide an answer that suggests your contact needs to change or at least will present the opportunity to explore something new, because that will also cause them to recognize their approach is One-Down.

Let me ask you a question you will have trouble answering: "What questions do you ask your clients knowing that they don't know the answer?"

Here is a set of example questions you can convert to your industry:

- What changes have you made over the last twelve months, and how much have they contributed to your results?
- Are you aware of any new approaches your competitors have adopted that you believe are interesting enough to explore, or is that difficult for you to know?
- Do you know how your results measure up against the industry benchmarks, and if not, would you want to see an analysis?
- What new initiatives are in place to ensure your profitability as this new legislation takes effect in the coming months?

Remember, the game is "I know something you don't know." When you ask the question without feeling the need to immediately offer your contact a lifeline, you force them to recognize that they are One-Down. Don't overplay your hand by prosecuting your contacts with a flurry of questions they can't answer; even if they recognize your One-Up status, they will likely get upset and will find someone else to help them improve their outcomes. Simply expose that they are One-Down and move forward in the conversation.

Other questions offer inconvenient truths. These questions expose a gap in your contact's efforts, perhaps even negligence. You want to be careful here as well, as it's easy to overdo them.

- When was the last time you updated your standard operating procedure here, and if there was a better way to do this would you be interested in seeing it?
- Do you have a guess at how much the inefficiency might be costing you and how fast you could get a return on an investment that would improve your efficiency?

More is not better here. Once you help your client recognize that you are One-Up, you need not reiterate it. The art here is to do this with a single question if possible, something I sought to do earlier by asking you what questions you ask your clients knowing they can't provide an answer. It's important to remember that you are only showing the gap in knowledge and experience so you can correct it.

You are not trying to prove you are a superior human, so stay away from questions like, "Did you and I meet when I was getting my MBA at Yale?" That kind of question may well suggest that you know something your contact doesn't know. But instead of giving them hope that you can help improve their results, it is designed to make them feel self-conscious and inferior, something you should never do in sales—or in any other situation.

How to Control the Sales Conversation

Earlier in this book, you learned how to deal with an RFP by calling the person who let it, then informing them that there was something wrong with their overall approach or that their questions are outdated and prevent you from providing them with a better way to improve their outcomes. Employing this approach is an execution of "I know something you don't know."

The salesperson and their client often have a contest over who leads the sales conversation outside of a formal request for a proposal. The conflict you experience here is one where your client believes their process is greater than your vantage point, the experience, and knowledge you possess about how best to pursue their goals and initiatives.

It's not uncommon to hear a salesperson complain that their prospect ghosted them after they presented their proposal and pricing. When asked how it was possible that they presented and proposed but the client sat there saying nothing at all, they confess that they emailed the proposal and the pricing, giving up control of the process and allowing the prospect to avoid the conversations that would have provided them more help. You and your client are both going to suffer negative outcomes when you allow them to treat the process as transactional: You lose the deal, and your client does not get the best outcomes you might have provided.

Again, anytime you experience a problem, you need to pro-actively do something about it earlier in the conversation. Here, there are questions you can ask that expose that your client is missing information and insights.

The first question is a bit of a tie-down, but not one that creates pressure. Instead, it communicates that you're so familiar with your client's options that you can bypass the bad ones and go right to a better approach: "Would it be okay if I share with you what works best for most people when exploring the change you are considering now?"

You make it difficult to say no when you ask to share what works, because there is no reason not to know what works for others and it doesn't obligate you to anything that would raise a red flag. The question, however, positions you as the person who knows best how to pursue the better results the prospective client needs, so naturally they will ask you what you would recommend. Here's where your answer puts your client in a bit of a box:

> What works best is that we have a conversation about the results you are pursuing and how to deal with the forces that cause poor results. From there, we'll schedule a meeting with the people in your company who are going to need to

participate in exploring what might work, along with anyone whose support you are going to need, including the person who will be signing a contract. At this point, you'll have a better idea what you want, but we're not quite to the decision yet. As part of our process, we'll want to build a plan to make sure we get the buy-in we'll need from your team to ensure success. After we have buy-in and have resolved any and all concerns, you'll be ready to decide and move forward. Is there anything you need to add to this process?

Now, having told them what works best, you make it more difficult to refuse the process. By asking your contact what else they might need, you are also beginning a collaboration that includes them and their team as active participants.

Your clients can cause problems when they try to skip steps in the conversation. Sometimes they short-circuit the conversation because they recognize how difficult it is to change, instead exploring change on their own, with little willingness to go too deep too fast.

Zombie deals—those that are already dead but still look alive—are endemic to just about every sales pipeline, and they're the most detrimental feature to salespeople's results and forecasts. Most salespeople believe that the client decides on change at the end of the sales conversation, not realizing that most decisions are made earlier in the conversation. To ensure you use your time wisely, try asking this: "Does it make sense to pursue this change now, and will we be able to get the time, money, and consensus to improve your results?"

This question confirms that your contact understands that you are both going to work to move them from their current state to their better future state. Whether you win or lose a deal, you are always better off ensuring your client has the right conversations. When they say, "I'm not sure it's the right time," you can ask a question that's come up before in this book: "Does it make sense to do it on a timeline of your choosing, and what concerns would you have if you were forced to change at a time that was not optimal?"

There is a long list of conversations that clients try to avoid. Here are more than enough examples to know how to expose your contact's lack of experience:

- I am more than happy to share with you some of the ways we help clients improve their results. How important is it that we adjust how we do things to fit your needs?
- I understand how difficult it is to get buy-in from a team. What are we going to do when they resist the change because we left them out, and how will we explain any failure?
- Will you be better served by spending more and reducing your overall costs, or is the price most important, even if it increases your costs due to a set of concessions that have not been disclosed to you?
- It's a great idea to meet with your team to discuss this. How do we want to handle the questions and concerns they have that they'll need us to answer? I am afraid if they don't get an answer that helps them, they might not be 100 percent confident moving forward.

Keeping control of the sales conversation improves your chance of winning. When skipping past a conversation harms everyone involved—you, your prospect, your company, your prospect's company, and their clients or customers—there is no reason not to do everything in your power to prevent that negative outcome.

How to Level the Playing Field with Senior Leaders

In sales, you generally encounter two kinds of senior leaders. The first already knows everything and cannot take in new information, even when they would benefit from doing so. The second leader is open to learning. Because the leader who refuses new information is the real challenge here, we'll start there.

Here's one approach: "How important is it for you to compete with the rest of your industry, and what initiatives are you considering to catch up to competitors who have already transformed their businesses and their results?" If you prefer to provide a face-saving line of retreat (my strong preference), you might say, "I am certain that you want to compete with some of your competitors who have already transformed their businesses and their results. Can I share with you the three initiatives that will allow you to surpass them?"

It's important to know that senior leaders are generally concerned about making a bad decision due to a lack of knowledge and understanding. Know-it-all leaders pretend that they already know everything they need to know because their ego won't allow them to admit they're missing information and insights, a form of impostor syndrome. To prove that they're One-Down, simply ask, "What do you make of the data on this?" This is a very tough question because it exposes two areas where your client is missing knowledge and experience: the data itself and their ability to analyze it effectively.

Be careful when using these approaches, because an ego challenge can cause know-it-all senior leaders to recognize the game. Here is a softer way to ask the same question, this time making your client the victim, as if no one has shared the data with them before now: "Has anyone shown you the data on this and what it means for your results?"

Throughout my time in sales, I have found that the best way to disengage a leader's ego is to say something like, "I am sure you have already seen the data and have come to the same conclusion as we have; namely, that the way we have done things doesn't work as well as it once did." While I am more than comfortable with conflict, sometimes the direct approach will have much the same effect as trying to give a bubble bath to an agitated cat. That trick might cost you one of your lives!

Enlightened leaders are much easier to approach because they already know they don't know everything they need to know. They look for experts to help them decide. The reason the big companies use big consulting firms is because they want the protection of showing the board of directors the $3,000,000 slide deck they provided them, the one indistinguishable from the one provided to their rival and a dozen other firms.

To level the playing field, you need only to establish that you have a well-thought-out and experience-based vantage point. You can ask a question like, "Can I share with you our perspective, why we believe it matters, and some of the changes we believe our clients should make to improve their results?"

Your perspective after reading this book will include the following: the forces that limit results, why the client must change, how to avoid negative consequences, the changes your client should make, and the only way to produce better results. You have more than enough information to recognize that your senior-level leader is not interested in traditional discovery.

You must present as a peer, an expert, and above all someone who can analyze a situation and make sense of it. You must have a perspective, and I would argue for one that is provocative. For example, I believe that sales is broken, and I can show the data to support that assertion. You must do the same for your prospective clients.

How to Help Your Client Avoid a Bad Decision

There may be nothing more difficult than preventing a wrong-headed client from doing something they believe to be correct. Knowing the decision will harm your prospective client, you have to provide them with insight that might change their mind. When they are dead set on a decision, you will struggle to nudge them in the right direction. Try language like this:

Four out of the last six clients we have acquired this quarter made the same decision you are considering. Not only did their decision cause them to fail to produce the result they needed, but they also lost time trying to make it work, and they spent more money than they should have working to save their initiative. Before you decide, would you want to hear one of their stories?

There is a subtlety you need here. It's part of the certainty sequence, a pattern that helps your client understand why it's urgently important to change. To recap, the certainty sequence goes through the following stages:

1. **Uncertainty:** Your client feels uncertain about how to get the results they need. This is where you come in and guide the client through the rest of the sequence.
2. **Certainty of Negative Consequences (Threshold):** You need to make it clear that your client will suffer negative consequences if they maintain the status quo.
3. **Return to Uncertainty:** Feeling the pressure of urgency, your contacts feel overwhelmed and they worry that any change could make things even worse.
4. **Certainty of Positive Outcomes:** In this stage, you support your contacts to feel certain about how to make a decision to see positive outcomes.

You don't want to mention your competitor or their product or service, because you don't want the client to be responsible for the failure. You want to point at the decision and the negative consequences for the companies you have helped recover, in cases where you took a client away from your competitor. The word "considering" is also not an accident; it creates an emergency hatch the client can deploy after learning enough to know better.

What you should fear here is that if you fail to prevent the decision, some decision-makers may not want to admit you were right all along.

How to Help Those Who Refuse to Learn

One holdover from the legacy approaches in sales is always to start with "the decision-maker." Having sold when that strategy was effective, I can tell you that it was a whole lot easier and much faster. But now you will struggle to find a decision-maker, instead finding a group of people who don't agree on the problem, the solution, or the partner they believe will produce the best result. In my long experience in B2B sales, I have found that some leaders and stakeholders refuse to learn, and often for different reasons.

One client called me to get help with their peak season, but their financial incentives prevented them from changing. Others refused to change because they preferred to do things the way they've always done them. Others believed that their teams were simply complaining because they didn't want to work hard. In those situations, two strategies worked fairly well, though they did take time. Both of these approaches are closer to marketing, relying on reach and frequency.

The first approach is to apply internal pressure to teach the decision-maker what they need to know. When I briefed clients, lower-level stakeholders were often part of the discussion. They would often ask for the information, an ask I agreed to without recognizing its power to teach the decision-maker what they needed to learn. As the people responsible for producing the results, they referred to our data and information in internal conversations.

Without knowing it, we had created surrogates that lived in the same space with the leaders who refused to learn. For some companies, it was difficult to escape the implications: their team now understood the nature of their problems and recognized that their leaders were responsible. While I could not keep up the pressure personally, the people who worked inside the company could relentlessly point at the truth. Over time, these companies eventually changed, often long after they knew they needed to.

The second approach that worked well over time is an infinite drip campaign. The world we now occupy has, to put it lightly, an abundance of data. Because our technology provides more information than one can digest and does so at ever-increasing speed, it's impossible to pay attention to everything. Leaders, decision-makers, decision-shapers, and thoughtful people seek ways to stay abreast of what's going on in the outside world.

The "infinite drip campaign" is a never-ending update about what is going in your client's world, featuring messages every week or two that keep beating the drum for change. The frequency is a critical component, and because there are always new stories and new data reports, it would be nearly impossible to run out of things that point to the change your prospective client needs to make. This is another form of narrative warfare, and when you are the only person diligent enough and smart enough to teach your prospective clients, even long-distance, you will have no competition for your client's mindshare.

New Beginnings

I always include sample language choices and talk tracks in my books. I wanted to use language in this chapter that moved you a little closer to the line I have cautioned you not to cross, because doing so comes with great risk and often costs you far more than your deal. By now, you can see how easily you could step across an ethical line that would change the very nature of your work in consultative sales. You are not trying to humiliate your prospective client; you are offering to share your wisdom. You are not trying to exert pressure; you are trying to teach them something that will benefit them. It's interesting to hear salespeople describe the ability to ask good questions as a primary element of a consultative approach, knowing that few such salespeople ask questions that help their clients learn something by design—and not by accidentally bumping into the aha moment, indicating the client just discovered something about themselves.

Each book I have published seeks to move the reader ever closer to a modern sales approach, one that creates value for their current and prospective clients. My first book, *The Only Sales Guide You'll Ever Need*, is a competency model for modern salespeople. That book formed the groundwork for the books and the approaches that followed. *The Lost Art of Closing: Winning the 10 Commitments That Drive Sales* provides a nonlinear view of the sales conversation. Unfortunately, I had not conceived it as a facilitated, needs-based buyer's journey until much later. However, leading the client is clearly described with strong guidance. My third book, *Eat Their Lunch: Winning Customers Away from Your Competition*, is about competitive displacements, a euphemism for stealing clients. It contains my oldest framework, and one of the most powerful: Level 4 Value Creation. L4VC may not show up in this book by name, but it's definitely here in spirit.

Armed with a new, modern sales approach, you have the practical, tactical, and actionable guidance to help your clients make better decisions and produce better results. Use what you have learned here to help others improve their results—deploying your One-Up advice, your recommendations, your good counsel, and most of all your support.

The Modern Sales Approach

ELITE SALES STRATEGIES is the fourth book devoted to the exploration and documentation of the modern sales approach. Like the prior three books, *Elite Sales Strategies* provides a structure and actionable frameworks to enable a sales conversation that differentiates the salesperson by arming them to create greater value for their clients and prospects and increases their ability to create and win opportunities.

The Only Sales Guide You'll Ever Need (2016) focuses on the need to develop the character traits and competencies necessary to succeed in sales using a modern sales approach, and how to improve your mindset and your skill sets, including the new competencies of business acumen (insight), change management (consensus), and leadership (leading the client to better results).

The Lost Art of Closing: Winning the 10 Commitments That Drive Sales (2017) explains how to gain the commitments that move deals forward, the Trading Value rule that allows contacts to commit to the right conversation at the right time, how to facilitate the client's buyer's journey, and the decision to fear the real danger instead of discomfort, and offers a blueprint for winning deals.

Eat Their Lunch: Winning Customers Away from Your Competition (2018) explores how to become the value proposition, value creation, and the varying levels, how to command a meeting with your dream client, the strategy necessary to capture mind-share and a preference to buy from you, a more complete view of discovery, how to find a way to a deal by building consensus, winning with intangibles, why you need to be a 52% SME, becoming a trusted advisor, developing an executive presence, and how to build a wall of fire around your clients.

Find additional resources at www.thesalesblog.com/elite.

Acknowledgments

OCCASIONALLY, AN IDEA is so compelling that it takes hold of you and will not release you until you acknowledge its power. These ideas seem to find you in the most unlikely places and times. I was exposed to the concept of being One-Up while listening to an audio collection of Alan Watts, a writer and one of the people who introduced Eastern faith traditions to America. Watts read a magazine article about the concept of being One-Up into a microphone. The article, "The Art of Psychotherapy" by strategic psychotherapy pioneer Jay Haley, provided a better description of the desired relationship between the salesperson and their client, providing greater clarity on the obligation to create value that allows them to improve their decisions and their results. The concept says more than "consultative" or "trusted advisor," terms often misused, misappropriated, and misapplied, making it easier to understand the obligation it imposes.

The concept and the accompanying obligation are timeless. As long as there are people who need to make important decisions, there will be a need for people with experience and insights.

First always and forever, Cher, for her constant support and inexhaustible patience. Aidan, Mia, and Ava, for being who they are. Any positive character traits I might possess are the result of my mom, who found a way to transfer her values and discipline to me against my will. My dad, for asking me about my work and my progress on things like this book. Thada Larimer, Tara Iannarino, Jason Iannarino, and Mike Iannarino.

Peg Mativi, Geoff Fullen, Brandy Thompson, Matt Woodland, and the rest of my extended family in staffing.

My friend Jeb Blount, for being my partner on the OutBound Conference, as well as forcing Shannon Vargo on me at Out-Bound 2021. Shannon Vargo, for recognizing the value of the idea in this book after watching the keynote and allowing me the freedom to write it. Christina Verigan, for helping me sort out the chapters and for improving the structure. John Acker, my faithful editor, who has edited over five hundred thousand words over our time working together. Sally Baker, Deborah Schindlar, Amy Handy, who had the last look at every word, and the rest of the team at Wiley.

Beth Mastre, Heather May, Francesco Lazzaro, Damian Wohrer, Dave Gardner, Bob Cabarcas, Amber Hersch, Nick Romanowski, Zach Hoover, and Austin Dunn, Chris Champagne, Kevin Barber, Tyler Naples, Giles Talbot, Samantha Murillo, and Stephen Coursen.

Because of the nature of this book, there was only one person to turn to for the foreword: Charles H. Green. Charlie's work on *Trusted Advisor, Trust-Based Selling,* and *The Trusted Advisor Fieldbook* makes him the best person to provide the context for the journey that follows, especially the ethical underpinning. I am grateful Charlie said yes.

About the Author

Anthony Iannarino is a writer, a best-selling author, a speaker, a sales leader, and an entrepreneur. His primary focus is human effectiveness in sales, management, leadership, and personal and professional transformation. Anthony publishes a daily post on his blog at www.thesalesblog.com, a practice he has kept since the end of 2009.

Index